"Preparing expository sermons—in  o
sermon—can at times be a tricky   s.
Yet, with the head and erudition o   e
heart and empathy of a pastor, and   .or,
Baxter employs the helpful metaphors of editor, reader, auditor, theologian,
and coach, to show us a clear and practical pathway toward more faithful
biblical exposition. Baxter's book is not just worth the read but more impor-
tantly worth the wisdom it imparts."

> —MATTHEW D. KIM, professor of practical theology and the Hubert H.
> and Gladys S. Raborn Chair of Pastoral Leadership at Truett
> Theological Seminary, Baylor University;
> author of *Preaching to a Divided Nation* and *Preaching to People in Pain*

"The pathway from exegesis to exposition often seems unclear and unmarked.
In *Preparing Sermons from the Page to the Pulpit*, Wayne Baxter provides a
detailed map for the journey. Preachers who want to follow the trail of the
text as they prepare to preach will find Baxter to be a most helpful guide."

> —RICK REED, president of Heritage College and Seminary

"Moving from exegesis to exposition, from the study to the pulpit, is no easy
task for preachers—especially novice ones. Wayne Baxter has created a helpful resource that leads preachers to accomplish this very goal. In *Preparing
Sermons from the Page to the Pulpit*, Baxter gives clear steps and concrete
examples of how to turn an exegetical outline into a homiletical one. Thus,
he instructs preachers to deliver sermons that are truly anchored in and
stemming from the biblical text without drifting into presenting sermons that
merely tickle ears and lack biblical rootedness. This book will be a valuable
resource in both the professor's classroom and pastor's study."

> —ERIC RIVERA, assistant professor of pastoral theology
> at Trinity Evangelical Divinity School;
> lead pastor at The Brook, Chicago

PREPARING SERMONS FROM THE PAGE TO THE PULPIT

Exegesis to Exposition in Seven Steps

PREPARING SERMONS FROM THE PAGE TO THE PULPIT

Exegesis to Exposition
in Seven Steps

WAYNE BAXTER

LEXHAM PRESS

Preparing Sermons from the Page to the Pulpit: Exegesis to Exposition in Seven Steps

Lexham Press, 1313 Commercial St., Bellingham, WA 98225
LexhamPress.com

Print ISBN 9781683596875
Digital ISBN 9781683596882
Library of Congress Control Number 2023933386

Lexham Editorial: Elliot Ritzema, Elizabeth Vince, Katy Smith, Mandi Newell
Cover Design: Joshua Hunt
Typesetting: Abigail Stocker

To my wife Lu and our three sons, Ethan, Micah, and Jared.
I'm truly grateful for what we have.

CONTENTS

PREFACE   XI

CHAPTER 1: INTRODUCTION   1
The Problem

CHAPTER 2: KEEPING IT TOGETHER   21
Determining the Outer Limits

CHAPTER 3: DISCERNING THE BIG PICTURE   31
How Neighboring Words Shape Meaning

CHAPTER 4: OUTLINING THE PASSAGE   53
How Structure Shapes Meaning

CHAPTER 5: THE OUTLINE BEFORE THE OUTLINE   87
From Passage Outline to Exegetical Summary Outline

CHAPTER 6: MANAGING THE MINUTIAE   104
How the Text Makes Its Point Matters

CHAPTER 7: MAKING THEOLOGICAL CONNECTIONS   133
How the Text Relates to the Rest of Scripture

CHAPTER 8: BECOMING DOERS   156
Applying the Text Appropriately

CHAPTER 9: CONCLUSION   167
A Sermon Revisited

SCRIPTURE INDEX   181

PREFACE

I REMEMBER BACK in the '90s sitting in one of my seminary classes at Trinity Evangelical Divinity School in Deerfield,
Illinois, listening to one of my professors opine about how the
evangelical pulpit was weak. He commented how the preaching
emanating from evangelical churches was not expository and
was superficial. Pastors would use the Bible, but their messages were not driven by what a given passage had to say; and
those who attempted to "stick to the text" only offered shallow,
"Sunday school" explanations of it. What he found most dis-
couraging was that this was the case even in a metropolis like
Chicagoland. Despite the region having seminaries (like ours)
committed to Scripture and with robust homiletical departments, most of the preaching he heard from the pulpit in and
around Chicago was weak. And as the pulpit goes, so goes the
church.

Although I no longer live in Illinois, decades later my professor's observation has become my own. There are many reasons
for "weak" sermons today. One that few people talk about is
this: While seminarians and Bible college students often receive
adequate training in the original languages, they are unable to
take the next step—that is, graduates find it difficult to move
from their exegetical analysis of a biblical text to writing an
expository sermon. Many students and pastors perceive a gap
between the analytical task of exegesis and the homiletical task

of writing a sermon, and they are unsure of how to bridge this divide. The purpose of this book is to help pastors and Bible college/seminary graduates do that very thing.

One of the objectives at the school where I serve is to help students who step into the pulpit to preach effective, expositional sermons. Over the years I have tailored my second-year Greek exegesis class to align with that institutional goal. This book represents an expanded, revised version of what I do in my lectures. My aim for every student who takes my Greek exegesis course is for them to have a much better grasp of how to take their exegetical analysis of a Bible text and create from it an accessible and effective expository sermon. May everyone who reads this book benefit in the same way.

May Jesus Christ be praised!

Wayne Baxter
Heritage College & Seminary
Cambridge, Ontario
Canada

CHAPTER 1

INTRODUCTION

THE PROBLEM

I THOUGHT I had written a good sermon.

I was a young, studious, pre-seminary layperson attending a small church. Sid, our adult Sunday school class teacher, was going to be away, so he asked me to substitute for him. Sid's Sunday school lessons were really just sermons using a different passage of Scripture each week. When he asked me to take his class, I naturally adopted the same sermonic approach to the lesson. My lesson/text was the baptism of Jesus in Matthew 3:13–17:

> Then Jesus came from Galilee to the Jordan to be baptized by John. But John tried to deter him, saying, "I need to be baptized by you, and do you come to me?" Jesus replied, "Let it be so now; it is proper for us to do this to fulfill all righteousness." Then John consented. As soon as Jesus was baptized, he went up out of the water. At that moment heaven was opened, and he saw

the Spirit of God descending like a dove and alighting on him. And a voice from heaven said, "This is my Son, whom I love; with him I am well pleased."

I never gave my sermon—er, Sunday school lesson—a title, but if I had, it probably would have been something like "Righteous Living Pleases God." As had been modeled by Sid, I essentially worked my way verse by verse through the passage, with my main points being:

1. We need to live obediently. (v. 13)

2. Sometimes people in the church won't understand our attempts to obey God. (v. 14)

3. We must always strive to obey God more than we obey people. (v. 15)

4. We can expect God's blessing whenever we obey him. (vv. 16–17)

It wasn't a barn burner, but I thought I offered the class a solid message. Everybody in the class thought so as well. I believed (and still do) that my message was an accurate representation of the average, weekly sermon preached in the typical evangelical church: a verse-by-verse "exposition" of a biblical text with contemporary, personalized points of application.

A seminary education later, having studied the original languages as well as disciplines like Greek exegesis and hermeneutics, I now look very differently at that sermon. Generally, my sermon was, on the one hand, biblically correct: there are passages of Scripture that reinforce each of my points. And my sermon was theologically correct—that is, it fits well within the historic, orthodox doctrines derived from the Bible.

But while I sought to be expositional, I actually had not been. Although I had worked through the passage in a verse-by-verse fashion, my main points were not in fact rooted in the text. They did not really reflect the Gospel writer's main thrust in Matthew 3:13–17. At best they were only a very general, loosely attached application of the passage, rather than an exposition of it. I unwittingly passed off application as exposition. What was not obvious to me then became obvious through academic study years later. My academic training taught me not simply to ask "What," but "Why": Why did Matthew include this account of Jesus's baptism in his story? And why did he put it specifically where he does in his narrative, compared to where Mark or Luke placed it in theirs? Was it to teach his audience about the nature of Christian obedience? That seems unlikely because there are other passages that more clearly and precisely address obedience to Jesus.[1] Was it to instruct believers trying to follow Jesus about the negative reactions they might experience from others? Probably not, since other texts do this in better, more explicit, and descriptive ways.[2] Was it to illustrate how God blesses Christians when they obey him? Jesus's sayings in the Beatitudes (Matt 5:3–12) as well as elsewhere in the Gospel accomplish this much more pointedly.

My sermon points sounded good. They sounded biblical—especially because I connected them to the passage. But the best intentions do not an exegetically based, expositional sermon make. What I thought at the time was that an expository sermon was simply what homiletics professor Ramesh

---

1. For example, Matt 8:22–23; 16:24. Although the language of "obedience" does not explicitly appear in these two texts, obviously, when Jesus says "Follow me," he speaks of a comprehensive obedience to him.

2. For example, the so-called Missionary Discourse of Matthew 10.

Richard calls a moralistic message.[3] In other words, my sermon presented general truths, truths that find support from other texts in the Bible, but truths that were not derived from the passage in question.[4] In fact, my message was actually topical, only masquerading as an expository sermon. Sadly, too many preachers in too many churches find themselves sitting in the same homiletical boat of preaching moralistic or spiritualized messages. Why is that a problem?

THE TROUBLE WITH MORALISTIC MESSAGES

Doubtless, some pastors and congregants see nothing wrong with moralistic homilies. After all, they sound good and can be quite uplifting. But moralistic preaching suffers from very serious deficiencies. First, in most moralistic messages there are two heroes: the biblical character in the story—an Abraham, a Joseph, an Esther—and the listener in the congregation who is able to faithfully follow the biblical example.

Why is that so bad? Because the purpose of the Bible was never to extol the greatness of Abraham or Joseph or Esther or any other biblical figure. If we take the Bible's self-descriptions seriously,[5] then the purpose of the stories of people like Noah and Deborah and David is to reveal and to demonstrate the greatness, the glory, and the character of the one true God

---

3. Ramesh Richard, *Preparing Expository Sermons: A Seven-Step Method for Biblical Preaching* (Grand Rapids: Baker Books, 2001), 22.

4. Robert Chisholm (*From Exegesis to Exposition: A Practical Guide to Using Biblical Hebrew* [Grand Rapids: Baker, 1998], 223) describes this common characteristic of modern "biblical" preaching as "Good point, wrong text!"

5. E.g., 2 Pet 1:16, 20–21: "For we did not follow cleverly devised stories when we told you about the coming of our Lord Jesus Christ in power, but we were eyewitnesses of his majesty ... Above all, you must understand that no prophecy of Scripture came about by the prophet's own interpretation of things. For prophecy never had its origin in the human will, but prophets, though human, spoke from God as they were carried along by the Holy Spirit."

whom these human heroes merely serve. Therefore, like the biblical narratives themselves, sermons need to be theocentric or Christocentric in their orientation: God or Jesus Christ, God's Son, is the hero. When a sermon proclaims faithful emulation of biblical characters (e.g., "Let's dare to be like Daniel and be a bold witness for God"), it implicitly diminishes the Christian's need to receive God's grace to live faithfully. The congregation's eyes focus on being like the biblical figure rather than on God and the imperative to receive his grace into our lives. Thus, the typical moralistic sermon emphasizes human works rather than being centered on God and placing the homiletical stress where it belongs: on God in Christ and the grace he bestows on his children.

Second, moralistic sermons are not life-giving because they are essentially expressions of conventional wisdom or even self-help, motivational speeches. People need more than this. After many of Jesus's disciples turned back from following him because they could not receive the difficult challenge of his Bread of Life Discourse, Jesus described his words like this: "The words I have spoken to you—they are full of the Spirit and life" (John 6:63). Like the words of Jesus, the words of Scripture—because they have been divinely revealed, divinely inspired, and specially preserved—possess the power to instill new life in the hearers, and not simply offer sensible advice or sage counsel. To be sure, conventional wisdom can be helpful. But holy Scripture inserts God's life-imparting grace deep within us, thereby creating a lasting, life-changing (in terms of thoughts, speech, deeds, attitudes) experience that, when lived out in community, has the power to impact and uplift those closest to us. Additionally, moralistic sermons lack transcendent spiritual authority to speak directly into people's lives. Given the immense magnitude of who the church is (the covenant people of the one true God), and given the grand significance of what the church does (bring the gospel of Jesus, God's one-and-only Son, to the nations), merely human words fail to arrest, instruct, and commission the body of Christ. As a result, the church remains unable to fulfill its mandate of imaging Jesus in the world and reaching the nations with the gospel. Nor will Christians be able to live as faithful witnesses in the communities they inhabit. In the preaching of conventional wisdom, the voice of God remains far too faint and distant.

Third, moralistic messages perpetuate negative stereotypes of how to understand the Bible. Whenever pastors preach, they model for their flock how people ought to read and interpret Scripture. Preaching moralistic sermons models for congregations that the Bible is an easy book to understand. Sometimes it is. Sometimes it's not. Although much of the Bible is simple enough to understand—even children can correctly draw truths from its pages—large swathes of texts and stories continue to confuse even the most learned exegetes and theologians. This should not be surprising. The Bible originates from a completely different time period and from an entirely foreign culture, replete with strange imagery and expressions, and is read in translation to boot. Why wouldn't some of it be hard to understand? While some assume that what it says in English (or any other modern language) is what it means today—no interpretation is necessary—more often than some Christians care to admit, that is simply not the case.[6] Not surprisingly, moralistic

---

6. For instance, in the letter to the Laodicean church (Rev 3:14–22), Christ chides the church, "I know your deeds, that you are neither cold nor hot. I wish you were either one or the other! So, because you are lukewarm—neither hot nor cold—I am about to spit you out of my mouth" (3:15–16). In the dozens of times I have heard this text referenced by preachers, "hot," "cold," and "lukewarm" refer to a believer's spiritual state. "Hot" means the believer is zealous for God, "cold" means they are apostate; and "lukewarm" means the believer is nominally Christian, possessing merely a status quo

messages model for an audience that a person can make a text mean whatever it needs to mean for the sake of the listeners. What it says is what it means—but it can also mean something different if that is what the congregation needs. While there may be many ways that a text or story can apply to a person's life, the author did not intend for his text to be understood in a dozen different ways. He meant something definite by it. The exegete must work to determine that authorial intent.

Moralistic sermons also give the distinct impression that anybody can preach a sermon—that preaching should not be limited to "professionals." But based on the myriad of scatter-shot, self-help messages being produced across denominations, clearly not everyone can or should preach.

THE TROUBLE WITH SPIRITUALIZED MESSAGES

In addition to moralistic messages, many preachers run adrift by giving spiritualized messages. This occurs when the preacher spiritualizes a passage, most commonly a narrative. The story is used as a vehicle for illustrating a spiritual reality or basic moral. It's not about understanding the historical and theological significance of a story; rather, it is at best about trying to make this ancient, foreign-feeling story immediately relevant for the congregation; and at worst it's about taking the first and easiest exit ramp to writing a sermon. In my first semester at seminary, I wrote a lesson for one of my Christian education classes based on 2 Samuel 6: the account of David bringing the ark of the covenant to Jerusalem. I used the story to teach about setting

---

commitment to Christ. Without getting into all of the details, when those three terms are understood against the social-historical and especially the geographic background, it becomes evident that Christ is not referring to their inner spiritual states but their attempted acts of service or ministry. Examples of misunderstanding the words on the page like this could be readily multiplied.

goals and how to work toward them—which seemed fairly obvious to me at the time. The teaching assistant who marked my
lesson, however, said I spiritualized the text and claimed that
that wasn't what the story was about. I was angry and offended,
but he was right. Is that what the author of Samuel intended
to teach his audience when he incorporated this account, and
not other possible accounts, into his history? Spiritualizing a
text like that one certainly makes for a relevant message, but
one void of historical and theological depth—both of which are
necessary to help a congregation mature biblically, theologically,
and intellectually in their faith.

It is certainly understandable how untrained preachers (like
my twenty-three-year-old self) can preach moralistic or spiritualized sermons. However, churches are not (typically) led by
these types of individuals. The shepherds of the flock are usually
people who have graduated from seminary or Bible college and
have received formal training in the original languages, exegesis,
and hermeneutics to help them understand and preach Scripture
in order to equip the flock for the works of ministry. But moralistic and spiritualized sermons continue to abound from even
within this group of pastors, despite their vocational training.

TROUBLE FINDS A SOLUTION:
EXPOSITORY PREACHING

What is the solution to self-help messages that inadvertently
squeeze God out of the picture and obscure our need to receive
his grace in our lives? What is the answer to the absence of
divine transcendence in the community of believers? What
is the remedy for simplistic readings of sacred Scripture and
a relativistic approach to truth? The huge deficiencies inherent in moralistic and spiritualized sermons, all of which contribute to the spiritual lifelessness in the modern church, find

their resolution in expository preaching. It is because expository preaching is, as Ray Stedman notes, not simply "preaching from the Bible" but "preaching the Bible itself"[7] that it provides a ready solution to the malaise of moralistic and spiritualized sermons.[8] It is only in the Bible that the sound of God's voice—that "Thus says the Lord!"—rings out because, as Paul instructed Timothy, "All Scripture is God-breathed and is useful for teaching, rebuking, correcting and training in righteousness, so that the servant of God may be thoroughly equipped for every good work" (2 Tim 3:16–17). The Christian church has believed since its inception that the Scriptures are God's word to us and, consequently, preaching the Bible faithfully enables us to encounter the living God. Such encounters bring about life-changing transformation in the lives of the hearers and doers of his word—something moralistic and spiritualized messages are unable to offer.[9] Therefore, it's vital that we as preachers do all that we can to give our people opportunities to encounter God by faithfully preaching the text.

---

7. Ray Stedman, "Declaring God's Word through Expository Preaching," in *Inside the Sermon,* ed. R. Bodey (Grand Rapids: Baker, 1990), 201.

8. Walter Liefeld (*New Testament Exposition: From Text to Sermon* [Grand Rapids: Zondervan, 1989], 20–21) helpfully summarizes what expository preaching is not: it is not exegesis, nor is it a verse-by-verse running commentary on a passage (a problem that plagues many pastors who claim to preach expositionally), nor is it merely a captioned survey of a text, similar to headings that appear over chunks of text in some modern Bible translations. Rather, an expository or expositional sermon could be described as a message that emerges directly and demonstrably from and is thereby constrained by the passage of Scripture being preached. Thus, the point of the text is the point of an expository sermon: no more, no less.

9. While moralistic sermons model a poor and superficial hermeneutic for understanding Scripture, D. A. Carson recognizes that expository preaching "*teaches people how to read their Bibles.* Especially if you're preaching a long passage, expository preaching teaches people how to think through a passage, how to understand and apply God's Word to their lives" (Carson, "Accept no substitutes," *Leadership* [1996]: 88, emphasis his).

What, then, can be done for seminary- or Bible-college-educated pastors who find it difficult to faithfully and effectively preach God's word to the people entrusted to their care?

ASSEMBLING THE PUZZLE

During an interview, three-time Grand Slam tennis tournament winner Stan Wawrinka said, "Coaching is very complex, it's like a puzzle and many things need to come together to make it work."[10] Of the many different comparisons people use to describe the process of writing a sermon, one analogy that rarely gets mentioned is that of a puzzle. Writing a sermon is like putting together a huge jigsaw puzzle. Everything is there before the task begins: all the pieces required to assemble it, as well as the box cover that gives the picture and final goal to work toward. But the task is rarely easy. It is sometimes confusing and often frustrating. Preachers have received training in the original languages as well as in the adjacent disciplines. They have taken preaching classes. They have even watched and heard enough expository sermons to know what theirs should look and sound like. But sadly, their messages end up becoming more topical than text-driven, and more scattershot and overrun with historical and exegetical data than singularly focused sermons. How can an exegete move from sitting in the middle of disparate puzzle pieces in the study to completing the box-cover-like finished product in the pulpit? The aim of this volume is to serve as a handbook to help exegetes who preach regularly to write better sermons—specifically, as it relates to exegesis and the explanation of a passage (in the New Testament, especially).

---

10. Rohan Alvares, "I Can Be Stubborn but Coach Magnus Knows How to Push Me," *The Times of India*, September 23, 2016, https://timesofindia.indiatimes.com/sports/tennis/top-stories/i-can-be-stubborn-but-coach-magnus-knows-how-to-push-me-wawrinka/articleshow/54475665.cms.

This book, then, does not discuss the field of homiletics, which deals with the rhetoric and the oral delivery of a sermon. That would perhaps be the next step, but one that I will leave to more capable orators. Nor do I focus on how to do biblical exegesis—the necessary building blocks for expository sermons. That would, I suppose, be the prequel to the present volume. Here I want to help the reader transition from the foundation of the exegetical analysis to the edifice of the message.

After pastoring for a decade, I assumed a teaching post at Heritage College & Seminary in Cambridge, Ontario. When I first began teaching Greek exegesis, I adopted the curriculum that was already in place: pretty solid, standard stuff among evangelical seminaries. But over the years, I came to see that I was teaching the elements of Greek exegesis in a way that was disconnected from biblical preaching. One of our school's institutional goals is to help students reach the objective of becoming capable Bible expositors, and my course was not doing that. I was giving my students the requisite parts for the task of Greek exegesis, but I was not showing them how to pull it all together for writing a sermon. And inevitably, when students are taught exegesis in this way, after graduation some all too frequently shelve most of what they have learned and resort to writing topical and moralistic messages rather than expositional ones. Years ago, Old Testament scholar Walter Kaiser made a similar observation:

> Students [have been taught] how to parse the verbs; to identify grammatical forms in Hebrew, Aramaic, and Greek ... to analyze the passage historically and critically ... [yet] the very discipline that should have mapped out the route from exegesis to proclamation has traditionally narrowed its concerns too severely. As

a result, exegesis has been the one subject most quickly jettisoned by pastors in the pulpit.[11]

Many graduates disenfranchised with the study of exegesis resort to preaching messages only loosely related to the passage, often substituting application for exposition (rather than offering both). For others, their sermons suffer from information overload, thereby becoming convoluted history lessons that are confusing, hard to follow, and pack very little spiritual-nutritional punch. Obviously, neither of these scenarios is desirable for the church to flourish.

So, I began to reverse engineer my course. I still used the same curriculum, studying the same grammatical components of the language. But I began to make explicit ties between the various elements of Greek exegesis and sermon writing. That is when I started to see my students experience the proverbial light-bulb moment. This book in large part represents how I showed my students how to make those vital connections between Greek exegesis and sermon writing.[12]

When it comes to writing a sermon, I have found it helpful, first of all, to think of *the exegete as an editor*. The average feature film in North America runs somewhere between ninety minutes to two hours in length. The ratio of the total time spent filming the movie to the running time of the finished product is called the "shooting ratio," and it can range anywhere from 30:1 to 250:1. In other words, for the average two-hour

---

11. Walter Kaiser, *Toward an Exegetical Theology: Biblical Exegesis for Preaching and Teaching* (Grand Rapids: Baker, 1981), 20.

12. Kaiser, for his part, claims that the key to solving this problem is what he calls "theological exegesis." While the theological dimension of exegesis remains an important part of the process, and is discussed in chapter seven below, the solution to the problem of "the current famine of the Word of God" (as Kaiser puts it) begins much earlier in the exegetical process rather than at the end.

movie, between sixty to five hundred hours of footage is shot but gets cut, never making it into the feature film. Similarly, most of the work that goes into writing a thirty-five-minute sermon is left on the cutting room floor of the exegete's study. For any given passage, many socio-historical facts, numerous word studies, a lot of grammatical observations, and various theological insights never see the light of day in a sermon. And that's exactly how it's supposed to be! Nothing is wrong when many of your grammatical and exegetical observations do not find a place to nestle in your sermon. Exegetes must be able to rigorously edit their detailed study of a text. All of your insights cannot possibly make the final cut—nor should they. Less seasoned exegetes assume that they need to "show all of their work" to the congregation, either to demonstrate (or perhaps even flaunt) their Bible knowledge or to justify their employment (or salary). In moving from exegetical analysis to sermon exposition, you will need to learn and grow in this essential discipline of content editing.

Besides the underappreciated task of editing, the puzzle of sermon writing is composed of several different sorts of puzzle pieces. This book shall discuss four of these in some detail.[13] The first type of puzzle piece concerns the art and discipline of reading the text. Thus, we will examine *the exegete as a reader*. As twenty-first-century moderns, we all too often try to race to the end of whatever we are doing, exercising very little patience

---

13. The two categories of puzzle pieces not discussed include, first, *the exegete as a worshiper*. God preserved the Scriptures for us that we might draw near to him in worship with our minds and hearts. Writing and delivering a sermon remains fundamentally an act of worship: for the preacher and for the church. The other kind of puzzle piece omitted deals with the original context of the passage: *the exegete as an historian*. While the Bible was written for us, it was not, in the first instance, written to us. To properly understand how an ancient text speaks today, it is always crucial to understand first what the text said to and meant for its original audience.

for the task at hand, in order to jump (often illegitimately) to the end. So too in sermon preparation, exegetes rush through the all-important discipline of reading the sacred text—having been enabled to hurry through this step by our prior biblical and theological knowledge of or familiarity with the passage—in order to get to the urgent task of writing the message. While sermon writing presupposes reading a passage, we sometimes forget what "effective reading" involves.[14]

A second kind of puzzle piece deals with the minutiae of analysis, which calls forth the role of *the exegete as an auditor*. Imagine if the love of your life left you a lengthy letter—the only direct form of correspondence you would receive until you saw them again many years later. How would you read that text? Would you simply scan it, perhaps reading only the first and last line of every paragraph to get the overall sense of the letter? Or would you pore over the letter, sentence by sentence, word by word? God has given his church a written text—a true revelation of himself—so that we might pay it the close and careful attention it rightly deserves, something we strive to do out of our devotion to him.

A third type of puzzle piece I discuss involves integrating the specific passage into the broader current of Scripture, whereby we consider *the exegete as a theologian*. Whatever text is under consideration, it only speaks a partial word on a matter. That partial word can then be integrated into what the Bible speaks overall on that topic. This last sort of puzzle piece represents a move from exegesis to biblical and systematic theology and can help a church to mature biblically and theologically. But some

---

14. English literature scholar Karen Swallow Prior advocates for "'reading virtuously': [to read] closely, being faithful to both text and context, interpreting accurately and insightfully" (Karen Swallow Prior, *On Reading Well: Finding the Good Life through Great Books* [Grand Rapids: Brazos Press, 2018], 15).

exegetes move far too quickly to this stage and end up reading a lot of general biblical and theological truths back into the passage (called "eisegesis"), making the passage say things it simply does not say. Consequently, the proverbial tail wags the dog.

The final kind of puzzle piece focuses on applying the text to the audience: we consider *the exegete as a coach.* The God of the universe has spoken to us in the Scriptures, and through his word, he makes sovereign demands on our lives. The job of coaches is not just to cheer their teams on. They don't merely offer instructions to their players. They call each one of them to make particular changes: to omit certain actions or deeds; to add others; to alter the way they do some things; to embrace a specific vision in order to help them become better players and a better team. Likewise, the expository sermon moves from the pages of Scripture into the lives of the hearers through sermon application, wherein the preacher challenges the congregation to respond to Scripture, offering specific ways they can do so, in order to help them grow spiritually as Christians and as a church.

WHO IS THIS BOOK FOR?

Since my main objective is to assist you in moving from the building blocks of exegetical analysis to the structure of expository sermons, a certain kind of reader stands to benefit most from this book. While I have already identified this person generally, it might be helpful to offer a more specific profile.

This book assumes that the reader recognizes the immense value of and is deeply committed to expository preaching.[15]

---

15. Although there may be seasons calling for a topical message, in terms of the monthly rhythm of preaching, topical sermons should be the exceptions to the rule. The implied reader of this book does not need to be persuaded into a commitment to expository preaching.

This book assumes that the reader has not only graduated from a Bible college or seminary program that required multiple courses in the biblical languages and hermeneutics (or equivalent), but that they continue to deploy these disciplines as best they can when crafting a sermon. New Testament scholar Walter Liefeld makes a helpful distinction between exegesis and exposition: "In exegesis, one studies each part of the Greek sentence, doing careful analysis with a view to understanding each truth presented accurately. In large measure, this is done line by line. In exposition, on the other hand, the passage is studied as a whole, and with attention to the flow of thought or sequence of events."[16] While shortcuts are available to exegetes,[17] this book assumes that if the reader uses them, it will only be to check their work and not serve as a substitute for it. Nothing quite substitutes for a fresh wrestling match with the sacred text. While much can be learned from watching someone else (like a Bible scholar) wrestle with it, observation can never equate to practice. Maximum benefit comes from doing the hard work of exegesis, not simply by watching other people do it.

The targeted reader for this book is also someone who preaches from a pastoral perspective rather than from an academic one. In other words, you analyze the text, write the message, and preach it to an audience for the express purpose of helping them encounter God from the text in order to facilitate Holy Spirit-changed hearts and lives: a sanctificational encounter. The person who speaks on a passage from a merely academic perspective has no such goal. Their sermons can still prove helpful insofar as they are informative and enlightening— as the hearers can come away with fresh thoughts on a passage.

---

16. Liefeld, *New Testament Exposition*, 20.

17. E.g., various Bible software.

But this can never be enough for the shepherd of God's flock. Expository sermons must never devolve into mere information download. The chief end of preaching must always be a sanctificational encounter with the God of the text.

This book also assumes that the reader readily acknowledges the massive imperative for the exegete to locate any given text within its social-historical background. The words of Scripture did not arrive in a vacuum. Knowing who said something, when they said it, and about whom they said it matters immensely. The ideal reader of this book knows that when modern readers approach an ancient text, they stand in an interpretive gap created by the enormous differences of time, cultural norms, language, as well as any missing pieces of information stemming from the shared history and experience between the original author and his audience. This interpretive gap can only be bridged through the careful analysis of the social-historical context of the passage. Further, beyond simply holding analytical relevance, background studies can "turn a sermon from a two-dimensional study to a three-dimensional cinematic event."[18] In other words, examining the social-historical context helps the congregation place themselves in the world of the text to identify its relevance for the original audience, so that, as New Testament scholar Grant Osborne states, "we can then help the hearers to discover situations parallel to the text in their own life and to contextualize the principle behind the text for the current situations."[19] Therefore, the study of the

---

18. Grant Osborne, *The Hermeneutical Spiral: A Comprehensive Introduction to Biblical Interpretation*, 2nd ed. (Downers Grove, IL: IVP, 2006), 158. Osborne continues, "The stories and discourses of the Bible were never meant to be merely two-dimensional treatises divorced from real life. Everyone was written within a concrete cultural milieu and written to a concrete situation."

19. Osborne, *Spiral*, 180.

social-historical background of a text is the necessary first step involved in building the exegetical foundation for the expository sermon. This book assumes that the exegete has completed the requisite examination of the social-historical context surrounding the passage they desire to preach.

At this juncture, it's probably worth noting the fairly exclusive nature of exegesis. Some people in the church naively believe that, given the opportunity, they too could preach (never mind the famous stat that the number-one ranked fear that people have is public speaking). Most churchgoers readily recognize that preaching is a gift and, consequently, not everyone should do it (including some who presently occupy that ministry in some churches), and among those who do, some are simply better at it than others. But because it is also a skill, preachers can improve in this enterprise by diligently working at sharpening their homiletical skills. I believe this same perspective also holds true for the task of exegesis. Grant Osborne describes the enterprise of hermeneutics as both a science and an art (or one could say, "skill" or "gift").[20] This applies not only to the whole field of hermeneutics but also to its constituent parts like exegesis. Similar to homiletics, then, while every preacher can surely improve in the exegetical task through regular and diligent practicing of the elements of exegesis, some exegetes will simply be better at it than others because they are more innately skilled at it. And that's all right. But insofar as exegesis is a science to be applied, any exegete desiring to preach can certainly grow in this central area.

---

20. Osborne states that it is a science because "it provides a logical, orderly classification of the laws of interpretation." It is also an art because "it is an acquired skill demanding both imagination and an ability to apply the 'laws' to selected passages or books … [resulting] from extensive practice in the field" (Osborne, *Spiral*, 21–22).

To keep this study to a convenient handbook length, I have self-imposed four limitations. First, I focus on the process of moving from the task of exegesis to writing expository sermons. I do not deal with the next stage, which would be more homiletical in nature: transforming the exegetical results or observations into a skillfully packaged, rhetorically engaging sermon outline. That would be a different book. Another limitation concerns the lack of discussion of genre, that is, the types of biblical literature. Scripture is replete with diverse literary forms—for example, legal texts, narrative, poetry, wisdom, and prophetic. Even from the much smaller New Testament side of the Bible there is gospel, historiography, epistle, and apocalyptic; and within each of these macro-genres, there are units of still more genres: beatitudes, wisdom, proverbs, liturgy, and the like. Understanding what type of literature you are dealing with is vital to the hermeneutical enterprise because each genre possesses its own intrinsic purposes and rules for interpretation and must be treated accordingly.[21]

But as important as genre analysis is, I do not deal with it here for several reasons. On the one hand, given the immensity of biblical genres, analytical discussion of how to work with each one would unnecessarily increase the density of this book and weigh it down significantly. On the other hand, genre analysis belongs solely to the realm of exegesis, and while my book is concerned with the exegetical enterprise, its central purpose

---

21. Thus, New Testament scholar Graham Stanton writes, "The first step in the interpretation of any writing, whether ancient or modern, is to establish its literary genre. ... A decision about the genre of a work and the discovery of its meaning are inextricably interrelated; different types of texts require different types of interpretation" (Stanton, "Matthew: βίβλιος, εὐαγγέλιον, βίος?" in *The Four Gospels, 1992: Festschrift for Frans Neirynck*, ed. F. van Segbroeck, C. Tuckett, G. Van Belle, and J. Verheyden [Leuven: Leuven University Press, 1992], 1187). For an excellent survey of how to work with the different biblical genres, see Osborne, *Spiral*, 181–322.

is not the how-to of exegesis but rather the process of moving from exegesis to exposition. Additionally, academic commentaries—which I wholeheartedly recommend for exegesis[22]—are very attuned to genre analysis, incorporating it into their Greek or Hebrew exegesis. Hence, the exegete can lean on them in this area (as they can for assessing the social-historical background).

A further limitation relates to the original languages. The reader will notice that I work more extensively with the Greek text than I do the Hebrew. Full disclosure: as a professor of New Testament and Greek, my skills in Greek far exceed my ability in Hebrew; hence, the examples proffered tilt in that direction. The fourth limitation pertains to the examples I give to illustrate the various elements of exegesis. I could have offered a different passage for every single exegetical task, but this would only present the reader with a sliver of the whole enterprise. It would merely give an atomistic perception of exegesis rather than a more holistic perspective. To offer the reader a more holistic view, I routinely deploy the same passages to illustrate different exegetical observations, thereby illustrating the different angles of analysis for one text.

With the foundation of the message now laid—or rather, assumed—I shall set my sights on constructing the edifice of the expositional sermon, beginning with the contours of the passage.

---

22. For a list of solid academic commentaries, see "Resources" in chapter two below.

CHAPTER 2

KEEPING IT TOGETHER

DETERMINING THE OUTER LIMITS

PSALM 14 STATES, "There is no God." None of the English translations of this verse say, "There is no *god*"—meaning, as Scripture affirms elsewhere, that there is only one God in existence, the Judeo-Christian God of the Bible, and that anything else that people call "god" does not exist. No, it says, "There is no *God*." Does that mean that the Scripture has a secret atheistic agenda? Not at all—not when we consider the rest of the words around that sentence. The whole verse declares, "The fool says in his heart, "There is no God." They are corrupt, they do abominable deeds; there is none who does good" (Ps 14:1). Clearly, reading the whole verse can make an enormous difference to how we understand a text.

The importance of knowing when a passage starts or stops cannot be overlooked. When choosing a passage to preach, you need to determine the proper text boundaries to ensure you are capturing one complete thought, rather than a truncated thought or one whole thought of one passage plus part of another. Oftentimes, finding the upper and lower limits of a passage seems self-evident. But sometimes it is not, as is the case, say, in Galatians 2, where Paul moves seamlessly from retelling his encounter with Peter to discourse and explanation. At any rate, care must be taken not to cut a verse or two off from the unit to which it properly belongs. Knowing what constitutes one complete text unit will help you establish the authorial intention in the text. How do we go about figuring out the upper and lower verse boundaries of a passage? There are a number of ways.

CONTENT AS A BOUNDARY MARKER

Perhaps the most obvious clue to determining a text's upper and lower limits is the content of the text itself: the passage of interest is different from the neighboring verses and it reads like a self-contained unit of thought. For example, consider the first chapter of Philippians, which consists of thirty verses. It would certainly be possible for you to preach the entire chapter as one sermon, perhaps if you wanted to do a four-week series covering Philippians, where each chapter could constitute a sermon text. But the chapter does subdivide into smaller, coherent paragraph thought units, based solely on what the section is about:

- Philippians 1:1–2 is the opening salutation.

- Philippians 1:3–8 is Paul's opening remarks of thanksgiving.

- Philippians 1:9–11 is Paul's prayer for the church.

- Philippians 1:12–26 is Paul's personal update.

- Philippians 1:27–30 is the first of Paul's exhortations to unity.

These subunits, then, could either generate a main point for the sermon that encompasses the entire chapter, or a subunit could be preached by itself if you wanted to devote more than just four weeks to Philippians.

INCLUSIO AS A BOUNDARY MARKER

Frequently, an author will indicate a unit of thought with what scholars call an *inclusio*: a rhetorical device where the first and last verses of a unit are conceptually or linguistically parallel to each other. Thus, the first and last verses serve as bookends to frame the unit. For example, while commentators recognize the first eighteen verses of John's Gospel as constituting the prologue, verse 1 ("In the beginning was the *Word* [ὁ λόγος], and the *Word* [ὁ λόγος] was with God, and the *Word* [ὁ λόγος] was God") and verse 14 ("The *Word* [ὁ λόγος] became flesh and made his dwelling among us") form an *inclusio* with the repetition of ὁ λόγος as well as the conceptual parallels of Word-substance, Word-location. Thus John 1:1–14 would form a larger subunit within the prologue. Detecting an *inclusio* in narrative texts like John can play an important role in identifying the boundaries of a text.

In the first creation story of Genesis, Bible translations end chapter one with verse 31: "And God saw everything that he had made, and behold, it was very good. And there was evening and there was morning, the sixth day." Remembering that chapters and verses were not a part of the original text (for any book of the Bible), a closer look at the narrative reveals that the creation account does not end at verse 31 (which the chapter and verse demarcations lead modern readers to believe). The first account, rather, extends into Genesis 2. Genesis 1:1 states, "In the beginning, God *created the heavens and the earth*," and 2:4a completes the *inclusio*: "These are the generations of *the heavens and the earth when they were created."* The second, close-up creation story, then, begins in Genesis 2:4b. Therefore, to preach the entire first creation account in one sermon, the lower boundary would need to extend to 2:4a—as the biblical author's *inclusio* indicates.

NARRATIVE FEATURES AS BOUNDARY MARKERS

When it comes to narrative, authors will typically signify a unit shift through changes in time, location, setting, or character. In Matthew 2, the different setting for each of the paragraphs indicates the textual boundaries within the chapter: the visitation of the magi in verses 1–12 takes place around Bethlehem, verses 13–18 describe the flight of Jesus's family to Egypt, and verses 19–23 record their return to the land of Israel. If you wanted to preach the entirety of chapter 2, each of these scenes or sections could generate a main point for the sermon. If, however, you wanted to park on chapter two for several Sundays, then each scene/section could constitute its own sermon text. Or, consecutive subunits could be combined for a sermon; for example, verses 1–12 plus verses 13–18 (i.e., 2:1–18) could comprise a sermon text, or perhaps 2:13–23.

Geographical scene changes also demarcate the subsections in Genesis 12, the call of Abram: in 12:1–4, Abram is in Haran;[1] in verses 4–9, the patriarch travels throughout Canaan; in verses 10–20, he is in Egypt. In the preaching of Genesis 12, each of these units could comprise a main point in the sermon.

Changes in characters signal the different subunits in the opening chapters of 1 Samuel. The narrative begins with Elkanah, Hannah, and Eli (1:1–20); then Samuel gets added in verses 21–28. The first part of the second chapter focuses on

---

1. Cf. Gen 11:31–32.

Hannah (2:1–10), moving to Eli's sons and their father (2:12–26) before closing out the chapter with the account of the man of God and Eli (2:27–36), followed by God's calling of Samuel that features Samuel and Eli in 1 Samuel 3. Once again, each of these scenes could generate a sermon text, or these subunits could be combined to form a larger passage for the sermon.

CATCHWORDS AS BOUNDARY MARKERS

Another way a biblical author can indicate the boundaries of a text is by using certain catchwords or transitional conjunctions like "therefore," "and," "but," "now," or "then." In the middle warning passage of Hebrews, the *inclusio* of 5:11 and 6:12 indicates that the unit of thought begins in 5:11 and finishes in 6:12.[2] The use of δίο ("therefore") in 6:1 would signal the start of a new subunit, to be distinguished from 5:11–14.

In a passage that Jesus applies to the Pharisees and Paul quotes to the Corinthians, the prophet Isaiah preached:

> And the Lord said: "Because this people draw near with their mouth and honor me with their lips, while their hearts are far from me, and their fear of me is a commandment taught by men, therefore (לכן), behold, I will again do wonderful things with this people, with wonder upon wonder; and the wisdom of their wise men shall perish, and the discernment of their discerning men shall be hidden." (Isa 29:13–14)

While both verses together constitute God's rebuke of Israel, לכן ("therefore") indicates the end of one subunit (the human cause) and the beginning of a second (the divine effect).

---

2. 5:11 has νωθροὶ γεγόνατε and 6:12 contains νωθροὶ γένησθε.

Near the end of Paul's exposition of freedom and contrast between believers in Christ and people living under the authority of the Mosaic law, he concludes in Galatians 4:28–5:1:

> Now (δέ) you, brothers and sisters, like Isaac, are children of promise. At that time the son born according to the flesh persecuted the son born by the power of the Spirit. It is the same now. But what does Scripture say? "Get rid of the slave woman and her son, for the slave woman's son will never share in the inheritance with the free woman's son." Therefore (διό), brothers and sisters, we are not children of the slave woman, but of the free woman. It is for freedom that Christ has set us free. Stand firm, then (οὖν), and do not let yourselves be burdened again by a yoke of slavery.

Paul's use of δέ ("now") in verse 28 indicates that verse 28 represents the interpretive application he draws from the citation of Isaiah 54:1 in the previous verse. The διό ("therefore") in verse 31 signals the concluding thought to Paul's argument in the preceding verses. The first part of 5:1 reinforces his conclusion, while 5:1b with οὖν ("then") marks a transition to the next, new thought unit in Galatians 5:2–15. Phrases like διὰ τοῦτο ("for this reason"), χάριν ("on account of"), or the common Pauline expression "I want you to know" also indicate new sections. By beginning his prayer in Ephesians 3:14–21 with τούτου χάριν ("for this reason"), for example, Paul refers back to the previous paragraph of 3:1–13. That 3:1 also begins with τούτου χάριν means that those verses in that section are also referencing the paragraph previous to it (2:11–22).

In some instances, a biblical author will use a catchphrase as a type of heading for a passage. Perhaps the most obvious example of this appears in the book of Genesis. The phrase

"This is the account of" (NIV) indicates the beginning of a new section within the book in Genesis 2:4 (the second creation account); 5:1 (Adam's descendants); 6:9 (the story of Noah); 10:1 (the descendants of Shem); and so on. Or in 1 Corinthians, Paul structures the back half of this correspondence according to questions the church had asked him in a previous letter to him (1 Cor 7:1a). The catchphrase by which he builds the subsections of the second part of his discourse is περὶ δὲ ("now concerning," ESV): "Now concerning … [marriage]" (7:1a) is elaborated on in 7:1b–24; "Now concerning the betrothed" (v. 25a) is unpacked in 7:25b–40; "Now concerning food offered to idols" (8:1a) is explained in chapter 8; "Now concerning spiritual gifts" (12:1a) is elaborated on in chapters 12–14; and "Now concerning the collection" (16:1a) is expounded upon in chapter 16.

VOCATIVE CASE AS A BOUNDARY MARKER

Other ways of differentiating sectionality include the use of the vocative case or direct address. In Philippians 1, the use of the vocative in verse 12, "Now I want you to know, brothers and sisters" (vocative case) marks off a distinct section from what preceded it, Paul's prayer of verses 9–11, and to introduce the next unit, his update in verses 12–26.[3] In Paul's injunction in Ephesians 5:15–25 to walk wisely and to be filled with the Spirit, the vocative appears in verse 22 ("*Wives* [vocative/direct address], submit yourselves to your own husbands as you do to the Lord"). This represents a new section of thought pertaining

---

3. Technically, Paul uses the nominative as a vocative here, as he does in the examples of Eph 5:22 and 25. Cf. Daniel Wallace, *The Basics of New Testament Syntax: An Intermediate Greek Grammar* (Grand Rapids: Zondervan, 2001), 35–36. Cf. Gal 1:11, where Paul deploys a parallel phrase ("I want you to know, brothers and sisters") for the same purpose of sectionality.

to the attitude of women in marriage, followed by a new subsection introduced by another vocative ("*Husbands* [vocative/direct address], love your wives, just as Christ loved the church and gave himself up for her," v. 25), which deals with husbands' attitudes in marriage.

RHETORICAL QUESTIONS AS BOUNDARY MARKERS

Paul also deploys rhetorical questions to indicate sectionality. His question at the beginning of Romans 6 ("What shall we say, then? Shall we go on sinning so that grace may increase?" 6:1) gets unpacked in 6:2–11. This is followed by another question ("What then? Shall we sin because we are not under the law but under grace?" 6:15), which he answers in 6:16–23.

CONCLUSION

For those of us who may be new to this process or want to compare their work to someone else's, there are resources to help you determine the textual boundaries of a potential sermon passage. Solid academic commentaries break down a biblical book into sections, with each section composed of smaller subsections or paragraphs.[4] Academic commentaries are written by legitimate scholars in the field (people holding a PhD from a fully accredited, globally recognized academic institution) who have accessed the primary social-historical evidence for themselves and who do all their analysis, including structuring and outlining, from the original languages. When in the New Testament, the United Bible Society's Greek New Testament or the Nestle-Aland edition would serve as another way to assist

---

4. It is vital that you use *academic* commentaries. There are different kinds of commentaries, each type with its own chief purpose and value: e.g., theological commentaries, pastoral commentaries, homiletical commentaries, and devotional commentaries.

you in the work of determining a passage's outer limits because the Greek text appears in unit paragraphs.[5]

With the contours of the passage established, the next step in the sermon-writing process is to examine the neighboring textual-literary context enveloping the passage to discern how the text is affected by its surroundings.

RESOURCES

Old Testament Commentary Series for Determining Upper and Lower Limits of a Text

Block, Daniel, gen. ed. *Zondervan Exegetical Commentary on the Old Testament*. 9 vols. Grand Rapids: Zondervan, 2000–2020.

Hubbard, David, ed. *New International Commentary on the Old Testament*. 27 vols. Grand Rapids: Eerdmans, 1976–2016.

Hubbard, David A. et al., eds. *Word Biblical Commentary: Old Testament*. 36 vols. Grand Rapids: Zondervan, 1983–2015.

New Testament Commentary Series for Determining Upper and Lower Limits of a Text

Arnold, Clint, ed. *Zondervan Exegetical Commentary on the New Testament*. 10 vols. Grand Rapids: Zondervan, 2008–2014.

Carson, D. A., ed. *Pillar New Testament Commentary*. 16 vols. Grand Rapids: Eerdmans, 1988–2015.

Fee, Gordon, ed. *New International Commentary on the New Testament*. 22 vols. Grand Rapids: Eerdmans, 1974–2014.

---

5. *The Greek-English New Testament: UBS 5th Revised Edition and NIV* (Grand Rapids: Zondervan, 2015); *The Greek-English New Testament, Nestle-Aland 28th Edition (NA28)/ESV* (Wheaton, IL: Crossway, 2012).

Hagner, Donald, and I. Howard Marshall, eds. *New International Greek Testament Commentary.* 13 vols. Grand Rapids: Eerdmans, 1978–2016.

Martin, Ralph, and Lynn Allan Losie, eds. *Word Biblical Commentary: New Testament.* 25 vols. Grand Rapids: Zondervan, 1982–2014.

Yarbrough, Robert, and Robert Stein, eds. *Baker Exegetical Commentary on the New Testament.* 18 vols. Grand Rapids: Baker, 1992–2015.

CHAPTER 3

DISCERNING THE BIG PICTURE

HOW NEIGHBORING WORDS
SHAPE MEANING

WORDS HAVE NO definite meaning by themselves. Words need other words to gain real meaning. Take, for example, the word "right." What exactly does "right" mean? The reader does not know what it means by itself. Does it mean "correct" (You got the *right* answer)? Does it mean "righteous" or "just" (Because of Jesus we can now be *right* with God)? Is it directional (I told you to turn *right*)? Is it referring to a prerogative or entitlement (We have the *right* to vote)? These are all legitimate understandings of the simple, five-letter word "right." But they cannot all be right … right? When other words, however, surround "right," then the term gains more specific meaning: *Lucille is very choosy when it comes to dating: she is always looking for Mr. Right.*

The same observation can be made about Scripture: to do exegesis of any given passage well, we must also examine the literary context—the neighboring text, the surrounding text that envelops the sermon passage, also known as the "co-text."[1] The meaning of a text is shaped by its neighboring words, or as Old Testament scholar Walt Kaiser so delightfully puts it, "Words, like people, are known by the company they keep."[2]

This kind of analysis that takes into account a passage's co-text comprises part of the field known as discourse analysis. Clarifying its place in the discipline of exegesis, Greek scholar Todd Scacewater writes:

> [Discourse analysis] is simply an array of linguistic insights that helps us understand what discourse is and how it works. Once we better understand discourse, then as we examine texts, those insights about what discourse is and how it works may help us to better understand texts as holistic entities (not as a linear sequence of sentences).[3]

Among other things, discourse analysis identifies the imperative to wrestle with the surrounding text of a given passage. It also recognizes that discourse has a communicative function: the wider literary structure does not simply serve as a placeholder for individual sayings; rather, it comprises part of the author's message to be communicated. In terms of communication, then, it is not so much that the whole is greater than the sum of the parts, but that the individual parts communicate through the whole.

---

1. Discourse analysts often refer to this wider literary context as the "textual context" or "co-text."

2. Walter Kaiser, *Toward an Exegetical Theology: Biblical Exegesis for Preaching and Teaching* (Grand Rapids: Baker, 1981), 106.

3. Todd Scacewater, "Discourse Analysis: History, Topics, and Applications," in *Discourse Analysis of the New Testament Writings,* ed T. Scacewater (Dallas: Fontes Press, 2020), 4.

While the previous chapter explained how to determine the upper and lower limits of a passage, a sermon need not be composed of only a single paragraph or thought unit. You can combine literary subsections: two or more paragraphs can form the basis of one sermon. Indeed, combining units enables you to cover much more of the biblical terrain in a sermon, keeping you from getting bogged down in one book for an overly long period of time. In this case, each paragraph might (though not necessarily) represent one main point in the message. For example, while there are many ways to preach the opening chapters of Genesis, one sermon could cover the first three chapters, whereby the first main point would consist of Genesis 1 (technically 1:1–2:4a; see chapter two above); the second main point would come from Genesis 2:4b–25; and Genesis 3 would form the final main point. But whether you use a single paragraph or larger swathe of text, you must always consider the wider literary context to preach the passage more effectively.

CONSIDERING THE CO-TEXT

Many preachers gravitate toward a particular passage of Scripture more than an entire book. Although New Testament scholar Gary Burge is referring to the whole of the New Testament, the conundrum he describes is relevant here: "We often explore individual passages of Scripture without seeing the whole. The individual passage is inspiring and easy to grasp while explaining the whole is far more difficult."[4] Looking at a whole book always takes more effort than simply focusing on one passage. There may be a certain text in Galatians calling out like a Siren, "Preach me!" and we are not interested in doing

---

4. Gary Burge, *The New Testament in Seven Sentences: A Small Introduction to a Vast Topic* (Downers Grove, IL: IVP Academic, 2019), 1.

an entire sermon series on the book of Galatians. How would you go about considering the co-text, that is, examining how the neighboring words enveloping the specific sermon passage affect the verse's meaning?

The Distant Aerial View

First, you need to read the whole book, preferably in one sitting, and more than once. After all, the only reason the sermon passage in question exists is because the book in which it appears exists. Without the book, we would not have the passage.[5] While there is a time for skimming, this would not be it. Karen Swallow Prior writes that "habitual skimming is for the mind what a steady diet of fast food is for the body. ... When you read quickly, you aren't thinking critically or making connections. Worse yet, speed-reading [merely offers] superficial knowledge and overconfidence."[6] When reading the whole book, ask questions like: What is the general direction of the book? What are key themes and motifs that stand out? Often, an individual passage will point in the direction of a larger theme(s) and/or bear some of the language that the author repeats throughout the book. A brief scan of Paul's letter to the Romans, for example, immediately reveals key terms that figure prominently throughout its pages: "faith," "righteousness," "justify," "gospel," "law," and the like.

The Close-Up Aerial View

Once you have thoughtfully and sufficiently read through the entire book, it is time to drill down deeper into the literary panel or unit section that the passage belongs to. Old Testament

---

5. Kaiser (*Exegetical Theology*, 77) calls this the "book context."

6. Karen Swallow Prior, *On Reading Well: Finding the Good Life through Great Books* (Grand Rapids: Brazos Press, 2018), 17.

scholar Robert Chisholm refers to this part of the exegetical process as "viewing the forest" before the exegete enters the forest and examines the trees.[7] While a close reading of the whole book can help you discern the subsections within the document, academic commentaries, with their detailed structural outlines, provide a convenient way to confirm or at least make this important determination more quickly. Individual segments of a book often have different emphases, which you need to identify because the specific section of words surrounding the sermon text shapes and informs the passage. The sermon passage is read in light of the unit section to which it belongs. What is the author's flow of thought leading up to the pericope being preached? What is (at least the initial) flow of thought leading out of the sermon passage? How does that text contribute to the overall flow of the author's thought in the wider literary context (co-text)? Walter Liefeld speaks of the need for the preacher to detect the "connective tissue" between a passage and its co-text because they "give a sense of direction like tire tracks across wet cement."[8]

Kaiser helpfully notes the different types of connections between the paragraph to be preached and its immediate context.[9] First is the historical connection, consisting of facts or events in space-time. For example, in the familiar passage where Abraham "bargains" with God in Genesis 18:17–33, the identity of "the men" before whom the patriarch intercedes receives clarification, on the one hand, from Genesis 18:1–16: their actions are described interchangeably between a plural pronoun, a singular pronoun, and Yahweh; Abraham recognizes

---

7. Robert Chisholm, *From Exegesis to Exposition: A Practical Guide to Using Biblical Hebrew* (Grand Rapids: Baker, 1998), 187–90.

8. Walter Liefeld, *New Testament Exposition: From Text to Sermon* (Grand Rapids: Zondervan, 1989), 32.

9. See Kaiser, *Exegetical Theology*, 84–85.

their eminence by hurrying (vv. 2, 6, 7) to show them hospitality; and they predict the birth of Abraham's firstborn son. Clarification also comes, on the other hand, from Genesis 19:1–29: two of the men are referred to as "the two angels" (19:1) who possess the power to strike the townsfolk with blindness.

A second type of paragraph connection is theological, whereby a doctrine may be dependent on some historical fact or circumstance. The appropriateness of the magi's question concerning Jesus, "Where is the one who has been born king of the Jews? We saw his star when it rose and have come to worship him" (Matt 2:2) rests on the genealogy of Matthew 1:1–17, which demonstrates Jesus's Davidic lineage and hence his rightful claim to Israel's throne, and also rests on his supernatural conception by the Holy Spirit (1:18–25).

Third, a logical connection comes from an argument being developed in the wider section. For example, the so-called Christ Hymn of Philippians 2:6–11 is part of the argument Paul launches in Philippians 1:27–2:18, where he explicitly exhorts the church toward greater unity in the body. The Christ Hymn would exemplify the unifying attitude the church ought to walk in to experience congregational unity.

A fourth kind of inter-paragraph connection can be psychological, where a line may trigger a parenthetical thought on the part of the author. Bible translators sometimes indicate this connection by using parentheses. For example, in Peter's speech in Acts 1:16–19, Luke injects the etymology of "Field of Blood," which the NIV indicates with parentheses:

> "Brothers and sisters, the Scripture had to be fulfilled …
> concerning Judas, who served as guide for those who
> arrested Jesus. He was one of our number and shared
> in our ministry." (With the payment he received for his

wickedness, Judas bought a field; there he fell headlong, his body burst open and all his intestines spilled out. Everyone in Jerusalem heard about this, so they called that field in their language Akeldama, that is, Field of Blood.)

To sum up: to preach a single verse on its own well, you need to take into account its co-text. For example, one verse in the Gospel of Matthew that offers a ready challenge for churches to live out their faith before a watching world is Matthew 5:16: "In the same way, let your light shine before others, that they may see your good deeds and glorify your Father in heaven." It would be shortsighted not to locate this verse first within the broader context (the aerial view) of Matthew: the Sermon on the Mount (Matthew 5–7), which itself is part of an even wider literary panel stretching from 4:23 to 9:35 (demarcated by an *inclusio* with these two verses) in which Jesus proclaims the kingdom of heaven through his words (chapters 5–7) and through his deeds (chapters 8–9).[10]

---

10. Matthew 4:23 reads, "Jesus went throughout Galilee, teaching in their synagogues, proclaiming the good news of the kingdom, and healing every disease and sickness among the people," while Matt 9:35 states, "Jesus went through all the towns and villages, teaching in their synagogues, proclaiming the good news of the kingdom and healing every disease and sickness." Cf. the very helpful breakdown of this portion of Matthew as well as the whole Gospel by D. Clark and T. Scacewater, "Matthew," in *Discourse Analysis of the New Testament Writings*, ed T. Scacewater (Dallas: Fontes Press, 2020), 32–42.

EXAMPLES OF HOW TO DEPLOY THE CO-TEXT

Considering the Co-Text of Philippians 2:6–11

Most Pauline scholars believe that Philippians 2:6–11 is an early church hymn.[11] Because of its complete, concise, and explicitly christological nature, preachers will often preach these six verses on their own, without any attention to the co-text. And given how gloriously the passage reads, it's completely understandable:

> Who, being in very nature God,
>> did not consider equality with God something
>>> to be used to his own advantage;
> rather, he made himself nothing
>> by taking the very nature of a servant,
>> being made in human likeness.
>
> And being found in appearance as a man,
>> he humbled himself
>> by becoming obedient to death—
>> even death on a cross!
>
> Therefore God exalted him to the highest place
>> and gave him the name that is above every
>>> name,
> that at the name of Jesus every knee should bow,
>> in heaven and on earth and under the earth,
> and every tongue acknowledge that Jesus Christ
> is Lord,
>> to the glory of God the Father.

---

11. See, for example, Moisés Silva, *Philippians* (Chicago: Moody Press, 1988), 104–6.

No preacher really needs to work that hard to make this text preach!

In terms of pericope boundaries, the Christ Hymn represents a complete unit of thought. While verse 5 could be added because the Christ Hymn offers the answer to the implied question in that verse,[12] to add a verse or two to the end of verses 6–11 would be a mistake and would upset the flow of thought. The Christ Hymn, however, could be subdivided into smaller stanzas (verses 6–7, 8, and 9–11) based on their respective content. Each of these subsections would represent either a main point in a sermon or perhaps even a sermon to themselves.

While this passage could conceivably be preached without invoking the co-text, important nuancing and even some relevance would surely be lost. After his opening, where he gives thanks for and prays for the Philippian church (Phil 1:1–11), Paul offers his "missions" report (Phil 1:12–26) where he updates his spiritual children on his circumstances in prison. Having already modeled for them a relationally inclusive and others-centered mindset, Paul goes on to demonstrate a gospel-first attitude that enables him to rejoice in the midst of his incarceration, on the one hand, and to rejoice despite attempts by others to exploit his imprisonment for their own personal gain, on the other. Because church conflict is one of the reasons why Paul writes Philippians,[13] Paul begins to address this issue explicitly beginning in 1:27. His exhortations to become a unified body and the attitude they must walk in to do so (1:27–2:4) find their exemplar in Jesus. The others-first attitude

---

12. In v. 5 Paul issues the command, literally in the Greek, "Think this." In other words, "Think this way," to which the audience would respond with: "Think what way?" Paul's answer: "The way epitomized by Christ according to vv. 6–11."

13. Silva convincingly argues this point in his commentary.

that Jesus possessed in his incarnation (2:6–8) must be fully embraced by the Philippians (2:5). And it is precisely because of his incarnation and his second coming (2:9–11) that the church must humbly work out their salvation for the good of their brothers and sisters in Christ (2:12–18). While Jesus is the ultimate example of an others-centered attitude, Paul also offers Timothy and Epaphroditus as further examples of this mindset (2:19–30).

The takeaways from a consideration of the co-text for 2:6–11 reveal that, against the backdrop of church conflict, the Christ Hymn has a very practical purpose: to show the church members how they ought to conduct themselves in order to move through their interpersonal conflicts in a more Christlike manner. Believers need to lay aside privilege and a sense of entitlement—as Jesus did—in order to serve one another. This important and easy-to-relate-to nuance would be missed if we focused exclusively on 2:6–11 apart from the co-text.

Considering the Co-Text of Matthew 2:1–12

The story of the magi's visit with the Christ child remains a popular homiletical choice for pastors before and after Christmas. Often the preacher, after offering the perfunctory sermon introduction, launches right into Matthew 2:1–12, concluding with, "Wise men still seek him, so let's seek him too." Clearly, verses 1–12 represent a full unit of thought, so it would be unwise to preach something like 1:23–2:12 or 2:1–14 because the verses immediately before 2:1–12 and those immediately after belong to separate units. But we can still gain a lot from considering the co-text of the magi account.

Matthew's opening line, "This is the genealogy of Jesus the Messiah the son of David, the son of Abraham" (Matt 1:1), essentially telegraphs his perspective of the incarnation. The Gospel writer's story of Jesus will demonstrate what it means to believe that Jesus is the Messiah (the Christ), how he is the Davidic Messiah in particular, and how he is also the son of Abraham. Each of these themes is large, multifaceted, and unpacked variously throughout his narrative. The opening "act" of the story, 1:1–4:11, explains the origin of the person and anticipatory work of Jesus the Messiah. This section subdivides into two smaller segments: 1:1–2:23, describing Jesus's origin, and 3:1–4:11, which depicts the preparation for his mission. The story of the magi (2:1–12) falls within the former segment. Matthew 1–2 consists of four units: the genealogy (1:1–17), the announcement of Jesus's birth (1:18–25), the visit of the magi (2:1–12), and Herod's plot and Jesus's safety (2:13–23). Chapter 1 delineates who Jesus is. The thrust of the genealogy is Jesus's Davidic kingship: he is the true heir to the throne of Israel, and he is God's true Son by virtue of his virginal conception by the Holy Spirit. Chapter 2 describes how people—the magi and the Jerusalem leaders in particular—respond to Jesus's birth. The magi come to worship him, while Herod and his courtiers seek to kill him.

Considering the literary context of Matthew 2:1–12 doesn't just demonstrate that the magi recognized Jesus as the messianic king and desired to worship him. Against the backdrop of the first four chapters, which showcase the person and anticipatory work of Jesus the Messiah, the account of the magi more specifically reveals Jesus's identity as the prophesied Davidic Christ-King whom Yahweh has appointed not only to shepherd Israel but also the gentile nations. The story of the magi brings all these different messianic threads together early in the Gospel in a way that they would not coalesce otherwise.

Considering the Co-Text of Ephesians 3:14–21

The second of Paul's two prayers for the Ephesian church gives us important instructions for experiencing spiritual renewal. In terms of pericope boundaries, there are several options. Paul gives a preamble for the prayer in verses 14–15, states the prayer in verses 16–19, then closes it off with a benediction in verses 20–21. So, the entirety of verses 14–21 could be preached, or perhaps the prayer and benediction (vv. 16–21), or maybe just the prayer proper (vv. 16–19).

> For this reason I kneel before the Father, from whom every family in heaven and on earth derives its name. I pray that out of his glorious riches he may strengthen you with power through his Spirit in your inner being, so that Christ may dwell in your hearts through faith. And I pray that you, being rooted and established in love, may have power, together with all the Lord's holy people, to grasp how wide and long and high and deep is the love of Christ, and to know this love that surpasses knowledge—that you may be filled to the measure of all the fullness of God. Now to him who is able to do immeasurably more than all we ask or imagine, according to his power that is at work within us, to him be glory in the church and in Christ Jesus throughout all generations, for ever and ever! Amen.

Paul essentially prays that the believers in Ephesus might experience the power of God's Spirit in their hearts so that they might know something of the limitless depths of God's love for them in order that they might become sanctified. Like with most biblical prayers, it's easy to dig right into the words of the intercession without paying much attention to its surrounding context. How does the co-text inform Paul's prayer?

Before launching into his prayer, the apostle introduces it with the words, "For this reason I kneel before the Father" (v. 14). It is "for this reason" (τούτου χάριν) that Paul intercedes for the church. If there's a specific reason why Paul offers this prayer, then it would be well worth knowing. It turns out that "for this reason" refers back to 3:1–13. But 3:1–13 also begins with "for this reason" (τούτου χάριν) in verse 1, so what Paul writes in those verses is predicated on what precedes them, that is, Ephesians 2. In the latter part of Ephesians 2, Paul discusses God's work of oneness—his bringing together of Jews and gentiles to form one people of God: "But now in Christ Jesus you who once were far away have been brought near by the blood of Christ. For he ... made the two groups one and has destroyed the barrier, the dividing wall of hostility ... to create in himself one new humanity out of the two" (2:13–15). This notion of Jews and gentiles uniting to form one unified people of God was unheard of. Some Jews did not believe that gentiles could even be saved—all that awaited them in the future was God's judgment. Other Jewish groups believed that gentiles could be saved, but their inheritance in the life to come was minuscule compared to Jewish inheritance. No wonder Paul repeatedly refers to this reality, only made possible through the gospel, as a "mystery." So, Paul begins chapter 3 by describing his own unique apostolic role in this divine work of joining together formerly separate and hostile people groups. On the one hand, he declares that he administers God's grace through preaching the gospel: "Although I am less than the least of all the Lord's people, this grace was given me: to preach to the Gentiles the boundless riches of Christ" (3:8). On the other hand, because the apostles believed their primary task was preaching and prayer (see Acts 6:4), Paul knows that he also administers God's grace through prayer. Therefore, he prays for the church (again).

This prayer, then, ought not to be seen simply as Paul praying indiscriminately for the Ephesians. His prayer is born from the work of the grace of Christ in the gospel, which unifies two previously un-unifiable people groups into one, and Paul's apostolic call to administer God's grace through preaching and prayer for the saints. Not only is the gospel the chief expression of God's limitless love for his people, but so also are the relational results of it: the uniting of Jews and gentiles in fellowship in Christ. And while Jews and gentiles are united in Christ, it nevertheless takes nothing less than the power of God's Holy Spirit working in the hearts of his children to enable them to grow in their experience of God's limitless love for them, enabling them to grow up into the fullness of Christ (sanctification) and to live radically: to love the previously hostile "other."

Considering the Co-Text of Job 42:1–6

The final chapter of Job consists of two parts: his prayer in 42:1–6 and the epilogue of 42:7–17. The entire chapter could form the basis of the sermon, or Job's prayer in verses 1–6 could be the focus. The content of the prayer is clear: Job acknowledges that God is beyond his comprehension, and because he spoke prematurely, without understanding, he repents before God. Still, reading Job's prayer against the backdrop of the co-text grants the audience a much greater depth for understanding the power of his prayer.

The first two chapters of the book introduce Job as a godly man (1:1), a rich man (1:2–3), and a family man (1:5). But he randomly—at least as far as he is concerned—loses everything. He loses his wealth to crime and to natural disaster (1:14–17). He loses his family to calamity (1:18–19). He loses his health (2:7–8). Eventually, even his wife turns against him (2:9). The bulk of the book (chapters 3–37) is composed of a lengthy dialogue between Job and his three friends (and later a fourth) who, upon hearing of this great tragedy, visit Job to comfort him. What began well (2:11–13) ultimately devolved into something of a shouting match: Job's friends continually blame him for all his troubles, accusing him of secretly and hypocritically sinning against God. Job, for his part, defends himself against their unfounded accusations. He also vents at God, insisting on an audience with the Almighty. Job eventually gets his wish, and God speaks to him in chapters 38–41. A survey of these important chapters—the setup for Job's prayer—reveals that God never answers any of Job's demands. Even though the reader knows from the outset the answer to the question of why all of this has happened, Job never receives an explanation. He knows no higher reason for why he suddenly lost his family, his wealth, his livelihood, or his health. Rather, God merely paints him a picture: a divine self-portrait drawn from the elements of creation. Along with this portrait comes a set of pointed questions for the patriarch—questions Job is speechless to answer. Then comes Job's prayer.

Against the wider literary context, Job's prayer reads even more powerfully. How can Job begin to understand why God has allowed his suffering when he cannot even comprehend God's acts in creation? Were God to sit down and explain to Job his suffering, he still wouldn't get it. It's beyond his tiny, finite comprehension. God's questions for Job demonstrate that the Almighty is not accountable to him. Suffering does not put God on the hook whereby he must explain himself to people. Rather, Job remains accountable to God, even for how he responds to and acts during his afflictions. Job's repentance, therefore, even amidst his trials, is the appropriate posture for this Old Testament saint. Job's prayer is certainly powerful and instructive on its own. Nevertheless, to cut it off from its co-text would drain it of some of its proclamational power.

Considering the Co-Text of Genesis 18:17–33

The eighteenth chapter of Genesis describes Abraham's surprise visit by three mysterious figures (vv. 1–15) and the patriarch's intercession for Sodom (vv. 16–33). While Sodom is the subject of Abraham's dialogue with God, both the previous and succeeding narratives make it plain that Abraham is really asking God to spare his nephew Lot. Genesis 18:17–33 is one of those texts in the book of Genesis that pastors love to preach: Abraham "bargains" with God and ultimately gets what he asked for. The text perhaps presents us with an example of how believers can "bargain" with God: Lord, if there are fifty righteous people in the city, will you still destroy it? What if there are only forty-five people? Okay, God, how about forty? Do I hear thirty? Twenty? Ten? These verses show us that believers should never give up when petitioning God but persevere when interceding. But what of the co-text? How does the surrounding context inform our understanding of this passage?

Genesis 12 begins the narrative of the life of Abraham. God calls Abraham ("Abram" early in the story) into relationship with himself, offering him a multifaceted promise composed of descendants, land, and universal blessing. The narrative then proceeds to describe various events in his life, including his sojourn to Egypt, his misguided attempt to realize God's promise of descendants through Hagar, and his receiving the covenant of circumcision. A fairly significant portion of the story is devoted to Abraham's relationship with his nephew Lot. It seems clear from the narrative that Abraham cared a lot for his nephew. When God commanded Abram to leave his father's household and his homeland to follow God's call to a foreign land, Abram took Lot with him (Gen 12:4–5). As their respective herds grew and it became increasingly difficult for them to coexist peaceably in the same area, they parted ways—but Abraham allowed Lot to choose his share of the land first. Lot chose what appeared to be the much better piece of property, leaving the old patriarch with the leftovers (Gen 13:8–12). Later, when a war broke out and Lot was taken captive, rather than simply forget about Lot and his predicament—which had no bearing on the fulfillment of God's promise to him—Uncle Abraham assembled a small band to rescue his beloved nephew (Gen 14). When the outcry against the wickedness of Lot's neighborhood of Sodom and Gomorrah reached God's ears, he decided to pour out his judgment on the city where Abraham's nephew resided, thus putting Lot in grave jeopardy (Gen 18:1–16). God graciously lets Abraham in on his plans, and it is Abraham's concern for his nephew's well-being that precipitates his intercession for Lot, though he never actually mentions him by name.

The wider literary context of Genesis 18:17–33 shows us Abraham's example of compassion and care. In fact, the patriarch became an exemplar for hospitality in the writings of Second Temple Jews (the "intertestamental" books) largely based on what he does in the story of Genesis 18:1–16. His intercession for Lot would echo this significant characteristic. He gains nothing from Lot's rescue. Lot does not factor into the fulfillment of God's promise to him. He does not need Lot. But he intercedes for him anyway, and the author makes it clear in Genesis 19:29 that Lot is saved precisely because of Abraham. This would represent, then, one instance of a nation (the one that will proceed from Lot) being blessed through Abraham in accordance with God's promise to him. Furthermore, while it first appears like Lot has chosen the better plot of land, it now becomes apparent that he has not, and that God's promise of land for Abraham remains unscathed by what will happen to the land of Lot.

Considering the Co-Text of Daniel 3

Talk about a chapter in the Bible that preaches! This one ranks right up there: its plot, the suspense, the courageous witness of Shadrach, Meshach, and Abednego, and King Nebuchadnezzar's public affirmation of the God of Israel. Who hasn't heard a rousing, stand-alone sermon on Daniel 3? What, if anything, does a consideration of the co-text add to this passage?

At the end of Daniel 2, King Nebuchadnezzar makes what could perhaps be construed as a profession of faith (Dan 2:46–47). He appears to have recognized the grand truth that Daniel's God, the God of Israel, is far greater than all the Babylonian gods. Yet this profession is short lived, as Daniel 3 opens with these words:

> King Nebuchadnezzar made an image of gold, whose height was sixty cubits and its breadth six cubits. He set it up on the plain of Dura, in the province of Babylon. ... And the herald proclaimed aloud, "You are commanded, O peoples, nations, and languages, that when you hear the sound of the horn, pipe, lyre, trigon, harp, bagpipe, and every kind of music, you are to fall down and worship the golden image that King Nebuchadnezzar has set up. And whoever does not fall down and worship shall immediately be cast into a burning fiery furnace." (3:1, 4–6)

It would appear that while Nebuchadnezzar had confessed with his mouth that Yahweh was "the God of gods and the Lord of kings," his heart believed otherwise. How else could he have instituted this vainglorious edict?

In Daniel 4, Nebuchadnezzar makes another declaration, but this one sounds different:

> It has seemed good to me to show the signs and wonders that the Most High God has done for me. How great are his signs, how mighty his wonders! His kingdom is an everlasting kingdom, and his dominion endures from generation to generation. (4:2–3)

In chapters 2 and 3 the king only issued statements about God, or what perhaps could be considered indirect praise. He does not address God directly but merely speaks about God. Similarly, at the end of chapter 3, the king declares, "Blessed be the God of Shadrach, Meshach, and Abednego, who has sent his angel and delivered his servants" (3:28a)—more indirect speech about God. In the opening of chapter 4, Nebuchadnezzar addresses God directly: he offers praise directly to God for what Yahweh has done for him.

Taken all together, Daniel 2–4 offers the reader a glimpse into King Nebuchadnezzar's faith journey. God was pursuing the king. He began this pursuit (at least, as far as we know) by speaking to him in an enigmatic dream in which God revealed the future of the Babylonian Empire to Nebuchadnezzar (Dan 2:1–45). We don't know exactly what kind of beliefs about the God of Israel Nebuchadnezzar had prior to this divine revelation, but after Daniel interpreted this dream for him, he confessed to Daniel, "Truly, your God is God of gods and Lord of kings, and a revealer of mysteries, for you have been able to reveal this mystery" (2:47). The third chapter of Daniel exposed the superficiality of his confession: Nebuchadnezzar had made a (kind of) faith declaration, but he did not yet embrace Daniel's faith or his God. Still, Yahweh continued to pursue the king. After throwing Shadrach, Meshach, and Abednego into the fiery furnace, Nebuchadnezzar saw a mysterious figure that he declared looked like "a son of the gods" walking around with the three exiles in the furnace, protecting them from harm. From receiving a prophetic dream to experiencing an angelophany (a manifestation of an angel in the physical realm), there is an escalation in the intensity of God's self-revelation to or communication with Nebuchadnezzar. As a result of this heightened interaction, the king issues a decree that forbids people from speaking against the God of the Jews (3:29). This is another positive confession of sorts, another step in the right direction, but Nebuchadnezzar is still not quite there—he still stands outside of the boundaries of a genuine faith-relationship with the God of Israel. In chapter 4, Yahweh ramps up his pursuit of the king by striking him with insanity, which eventually leads to Nebuchadnezzar turning to Yahweh.

Thus, while Daniel 3 presents a lucid story of faith and commitment to God in the face of steep adversity, when the co-text is taken into consideration, the bold witness of Shadrach, Meshach, and Abednego, within the Nebuchadnezzar narratives, also serves to demonstrate how God uses the faithful witness of his people to move others—even those in power—forward in their spiritual pilgrimage.

CONCLUSION

A sermon passage, then, is affected by its co-text, and the exegete must examine it to gain a better or fuller understanding of the passage in order to preach the text more faithfully and effectively.

Having examined the role of the wider literary context, we must now assess the pericope's own structure: the next stage in moving from exegesis to exposition.

RESOURCES

Old Testament Commentary Series for the Literary Structure of a Book[14]

Block, Daniel, gen. ed. *Zondervan Exegetical Commentary on the Old Testament.* 9 vols. Grand Rapids: Zondervan, 2000–2020.

Hubbard, David, ed. *New International Commentary on the Old Testament.* 27 vols. Grand Rapids, Eerdmans, 1976–2016.

Hubbard, David A. et al., eds. *Word Biblical Commentary: Old Testament.* 36 vols. Grand Rapids: Zondervan, 1983–2015.

New Testament Commentary Series for the Literary Structure of a Book[15]

Arnold, Clint, ed. *Zondervan Exegetical Commentary on the New Testament.* 10 vols. Grand Rapids: Zondervan, 2008–2014.

Carson, D. A., ed. *Pillar New Testament Commentary.* 16 vols. Grand Rapids: Eerdmans, 1988–2015.

Fee, Gordon, ed. *New International Commentary on the New Testament.* 22 vols. Grand Rapids: Eerdmans, 1974–2014.

Hagner, Donald, and I. Howard Marshall, eds. *New International Greek Testament Commentary.* 13 vols. Grand Rapids: Eerdmans, 1978–2016.

---

14. These appeared under "Resources" in the previous chapter but are mentioned again for convenience.

15. These appeared under "Resources" in the previous chapter but are mentioned again for convenience.

Martin, Ralph, and Lynn Allan Losie, eds. *Word Biblical Commentary: New Testament*. 25 vols. Grand Rapids: Zondervan, 1982–2014.

Yarbrough, Robert, and Robert Stein, eds. *Baker Exegetical Commentary on the New Testament*. 18 vols. Grand Rapids: Baker, 1992–2015.

Monographs

Duvall, J. Scott, and J. Daniel Hays. *Grasping God's Word: A Hands-On Approach to Reading, Interpreting, and Applying the Bible*. 3rd ed. Grand Rapids: Zondervan, 2012.

Liefeld, Walter. *New Testament Exposition: From Text to Sermon*. Grand Rapids: Zondervan, 1989.

Greidanus, Sidney. *The Modern Preacher and the Ancient Text: Interpreting and Preaching Biblical Literature*. Grand Rapids: Eerdmans, 1989.

Osborne, Grant. *Handbook for Bible Study*. Grand Rapids: Baker, 1979.

Runge, Steven. *Discourse Grammar of the Greek New Testament: A Practical Introduction for Teaching and Exegesis*. Peabody: Hendrickson, 2010.

Scacewater, Todd, ed. *Discourse Analysis of the New Testament Writings*. Dallas: Fontes Press, 2020.

CHAPTER 4

OUTLINING THE PASSAGE

HOW STRUCTURE SHAPES MEANING

IN SEASON FOUR of the popular British television series *Sherlock*, Mary Watson tries desperately to get away and hide from the great sleuth by arbitrarily adopting different fake identities and clandestinely traveling from country to country randomly to ensure her escape. Once, in Morocco, she walks into her room in an out-of-the-way hotel, only to find Sherlock Holmes waiting for her! She's amazed that he was able to track her down because, as she blurts out, her every movement was random. But Holmes smugly replies, "Mary, no human action is ever truly random. An advanced grasp of the mathematics of probability mapped onto a thorough apprehension of human psychology and the known dispositions of any given individual can reduce the number of variables considerably. I myself know of at least fifty-eight techniques to refine a seemingly infinite array of randomly generated possibilities down to the smallest number of feasible variables."

Human action is rarely ever truly random. There is always a reason why people do what they do—whether they are aware of it or not. When it comes to communication, people do not typically string their words together in haphazard fashion. We have conscious and even subconscious ways of emphasizing certain things we say. Sometimes the first word off of our lips has the emphasis: *Why* did you do that? In other instances, it is the final word: You did it *again*! Similarly, authors do not thread their sentences together in a random manner. When writing something as simple as a list, what is the order of items on the list? That would depend on the nature of the list and its purpose. If it is a list of top movies and it is being shared among friends, then we would likely put our favorite movie first and our least favorite last. Or because of recency bias, we might put it in a quasi-chronological order, beginning with our favorite film we have most recently watched. If it's a list of arguments in a debate, we might begin with our weakest argument and move to the strongest, or vice versa. Whatever way we choose to put our list together, it is rarely arbitrary.

There is a fundamental principle in language: main or independent clauses convey primary thoughts, and subordinate or dependent clauses convey secondary thoughts. A main clause is a complete thought that can stand on its own and makes perfect sense by itself. A subordinate clause, however, is an incomplete thought, grammatically speaking, and needs to be attached to a main clause for it to make sense. Imagine a cell phone conversation between a mother and her son. At one point in the exchange, the son blurts out: "I will come home after the game is decided in overtime." This is a compound sentence composed of two parts: a main clause, "I will come home," and a subordinate clause, "after the game is decided in overtime." The main clause stands as a complete thought: "I will come home." The rest of the sentence is grammatically incomplete: "after the game is decided in overtime." This clause needs something else for it to make sense. The main thought in the son's comment is not the state of the game—the subordinate clause—but rather that his mother can expect his return: he *will* come home. The main clause drives the sentence, while the subordinate clause merely unpacks the main thought: he will come home, but only after overtime.

This main-subordinate distinction is important for New Testament texts. Consider Romans 5:1: "Therefore, since we have been justified through faith, we have peace with God through our Lord Jesus Christ."

Here we have a compound sentence composed of two parts: the subordinate clause, "since we have been justified through faith," and the main clause, "we have peace with God through our Lord Jesus Christ." The latter clause stands on its own as a complete thought. The first part of the sentence—that is, the subordinate clause—needs something else for it to make sense grammatically. The central thrust of the verse, then, is not being justified by faith but that believers have peace with God.

The implication of identifying main and subordinate clauses for Bible preaching seems clear enough: whatever the primary thought is for the biblical author must also be primary for the preacher, and whatever is not primary but secondary for the author should not become main for the preacher. To make such an inversion would overturn the author's intended thrust or emphasis (even if the inversion preaches). How then do you determine what's main from what's subordinate in a passage?

OUTLINING NEW TESTAMENT PROSE

Of all the different types of literary genres in the Bible, outlining is especially beneficial when working with prose, which constitutes the New Testament letters especially. Outlining

New Testament texts must be done in Greek because, on the one hand, some words in English, like "but," for example, suggest dependency/subordination ("But she came over anyway") because in English we rarely begin a sentence with "but." In Greek, however, the words that most frequently correspond to "but"—ἀλλά and δέ—indicate grammatical independency. On the other hand, main and subordinate thoughts in Greek do not always transfer over in translation, even in literal translations, and thus their dependency can be missed. For example, Ephesians 1:4–5 in the ESV reads: "even as *he chose us* in him before the foundation of the world, that we should be holy and blameless before him. In love *he predestined us* for adoption to himself as sons through Jesus Christ, according to the purpose of his will" (emphasis added). The ESV translators have chosen to render "he chose" and "he predestined" as finite verbs.[1] This implies that they are equally weighted in Paul's mind: that they comprise two main clauses. However, in the Greek, only "he chose" is a finite verb; "he predestined" is a participle, which actually makes it grammatically subordinate to or dependent on "he chose." In other words, in preaching Ephesians 1:4–5, there are not two main points but one—"he chose"—with that one point having a subpoint ("he predestined").

In outlining a passage, the first step is to identify the finite Greek verb, that is, a verb form with "person": either first ("I," "we"), second ("you"), or third ("he," "she," "they") person. Finite verbs drive main clauses. With the main clause identified, you place it at the left margin. All dependent phrases will be indented to varying degrees to show how they relate to the main clause. In terms of independent/dependent clauses, then, the earlier example of Rom 5:1 would be outlined as follows:

---

1. I.e., as verbs having person—here, third-person singular.

Δικαιωθέντες οὖν ἐκ πίστεως

εἰρήνην ἔχομεν πρὸς τὸν θεὸν διὰ τοῦ κυρίου ἡμῶν Ἰησοῦ Χριστοῦ

Therefore, since we have been justified through faith, we have peace with God through our Lord Jesus Christ.

While each clause could be further subdivided,[2] strictly in terms of independent/dependent clauses, this is how Romans 5:1 breaks down. There is only one finite verb (ἔχομεν, "we have") that drives the action of the sentence. While important, the first part of the verse, which begins with a participle (Δικαιωθέντες, "having been justified"), merely accents the main clause found in the second half of the verse.

Independent Clauses

Independent clauses are often introduced by a coordinating conjunction—words like:[3]

- οὖν ("therefore")

- καί ("and")

- δέ ("and," "but," "now")

- γάρ ("for," "because")

- ἀλλά ("but")

- πλήν ("but," "however")

- διό ("therefore," "for this reason")

- ὥστε ("therefore")

- ἄρα ("then," "so then")

---

2. See the "Additional Modifiers" section below.

3. Cf. Daniel Wallace, *The Basics of New Testament Syntax: An Intermediate Greek Grammar* (Grand Rapids: Zondervan, 2001), 287, 295.

- ἤ ("or")

Once again, when seeking to identify main clauses, it is essential to think in terms of Greek, not English. Because of the Semitic influence in the New Testament, many independent clauses begin with καί, δέ, or γάρ. Main clauses in English do not typically begin with "and" or "for," but they do in Greek. To think in English while breaking down a passage into its constituent main and subordinate clauses hinders the process because there is not a 1:1 correspondence between the two languages. For example, while πλήν introduces an independent clause, in some contexts English translations might translate it as "however," which might suggest grammatical dependency.

Dependent Clauses

Greek authors create dependency in a variety of ways. Subordinate clauses are frequently introduced by the subordinate conjunctions ὅτι ("that") or ἵνα ("so that"). Thus, a clause beginning with either of these words should be indented to indicate its grammatical dependency:

> μὴ θαυμάσῃς
> > ὅτι εἶπόν σοι Δεῖ ὑμᾶς γεννηθῆναι ἄνωθεν (John 3:7)
> Do not marvel
> > > that I said to you, "You must be born again."
> > > > (John 3:7 ESV)

> οὐ γὰρ ἀπέστειλεν ὁ θεὸς τὸν υἱὸν εἰς τὸν κόσμον
> > ἵνα κρίνῃ τὸν κόσμον, ἀλλ' ἵνα σωθῇ ὁ κόσμος δι'
> > αὐτοῦ   (John 3:17)
> For God did not send his Son into the world
> > > to condemn the world, but to
> > > save the world through him.
> > > > (John 3:17)

While finite verbs indicate grammatical independence, when they occur within a dependent clause (e.g., within a ἵνα clause), they can no longer be considered main but subordinate. Hence, in John 3:17, while κρίνῃ ("he might condemn") is a finite verb because it occurs as part of a ἵνα clause, it functions dependently.

Relative pronouns like ὅς ("who," "which," "that"), used to introduce a relative clause, indicate grammatical dependency. Other subordinating conjunctions to look for in identifying dependent clauses are:[4]

- καθώς ("just as")

- ὡς ("as")

- ὅτε ("when")

- ὅταν ("whenever")

- ὅπως ("in order that")

- ἕως ("until")

- γάρ[5] ("for," "because")

- ἐάν ("if," "when")

- εἰ[6] ("if")

While distinguishing between independent and dependent Greek clauses is often fairly straightforward, this is not always the case. Sometimes the exegete must strike a fine balance between clauses that are *syntactically* main thoughts and clauses

---

4. See Wallace, *Syntax*, 288–91, 299–302.

5. Γάρ can introduce either dependency or independency as determined by the context.

6. These latter two words (ἐάν and εἰ) are conditional conjunctives.

that are *conceptually* main. Greek grammarian Dan Wallace puts it like this:

> Although the two elements might be equal *syntactically*, there is often a *semantic* notion of subordination. For example, on the surface "I went to the store *and* I bought bread" involves two coordinate clauses joined by *and*. But on a "deep structure" level, it is evident that coordinate ideas are not involved: "I went to the store *in order that* I might buy bread."[7]

In other words, clauses can be syntactically equal but conceptually subordinate. Context would be the determining factor. Thus, while γάρ ("for") introduces grammatically independent clauses, it can also introduce conceptually dependent clauses. Consider, for example, one of the most memorized verses in the Bible: "*For* God *so* (Οὕτως, γὰρ) loved the world that he gave his one and only Son, that whoever believes in him shall not perish but have eternal life" (John 3:16). That this verse begins with the combination of the coordinating conjunction γάρ and the adverb οὕτως ("so") means that, while John 3:16 is typically cited and memorized by itself, its thought is actually conceptually subordinate to the previous verses: "Just as Moses lifted up the snake in the wilderness, so the Son of Man must be lifted up, that everyone who believes may have eternal life in him" (3:14–15). John 3:16 serves to describe the lifting up of the Son (on the cross) as an expression of God's love for the world.

Along somewhat comparable lines, although ὅτι is a subordinate conjunction, and therefore the clause it introduces ought to

---

7. Wallace, *Syntax*, 294n2 (emphasis his).

be indented, the concept it introduces should not be separated from the clause it is grammatically connected to: conceptually, the clauses go together. Paul, for example, periodically speaks of knowing something as "I know that." Philippians 1:12 can be subdivided as:

> Γινώσκειν δὲ ὑμᾶς βούλομαι, ἀδελφοί,
>> ὅτι τὰ κατ᾽ ἐμὲ μᾶλλον εἰς προκοπὴν τοῦ εὐαγγελίου ἐλήλυθεν.
>
> *Now I want you to know*, brothers and sisters,
>> *that* what has happened to me has
>> actually served to advance the gospel.

Although Paul's desire that the Philippians know something is, grammatically speaking, the independent clause, it needs its dependent ὅτι clause to get the full effect of Paul's update. While he wants them to know what he's about to say to them, it is the content of what he's about to say to them—the advancement of the gospel despite his imprisonment—that matters (to encourage and teach them). Similarly, in Philippians 1:19 Paul writes:

> οἶδα γὰρ
>> ὅτι τοῦτό μοι ἀποβήσεται εἰς σωτηρίαν διὰ τῆς
>> ὑμῶν δεήσεως καὶ ἐπιχορηγίας τοῦ πνεύματος
>> Ἰησοῦ Χριστοῦ
>
> for I know
>> that through your prayers and the help
>> of the Spirit of Jesus Christ this will turn
>> out for my deliverance (ESV)

While οἶδα γὰρ is syntactically the main clause by itself—conceptually speaking—it cannot stand alone. What is important here is the content of what Paul knows, that is, what has happened will result in his deliverance. There are, in effect, two sides to the thought coin in this verse: that the prayers of the Philippians and the activity of God's Spirit will produce Paul's deliverance, on the one hand, and that the apostle personally knows this fact, on the other, which is why he can "rejoice" (v. 18).

In this way, then, ὅτι clauses, while syntactically subordinate, can sometimes fill out the main thought in the independent clause, thereby functioning like part of the main clause. But always, context will provide the final determinant as to whether this is the case.

Adverbial participial phrases such as Δικαιωθέντες ("having been justified," Rom 5:1) also introduce dependency and are used to modify the main verb:

> Δικαιωθέντες οὖν ἐκ πίστεως
> εἰρήνην ἔχομεν πρὸς τὸν θεὸν διὰ τοῦ κυρίου ἡμῶν Ἰησοῦ Χριστοῦ

> Therefore, having been justified by faith,
> we have peace with God through our Lord Jesus Christ.
> (NASB)

Similarly, Colossians 1:9:

> οὐ παυόμεθα ὑπὲρ ὑμῶν
>> προσευχόμενοι ("praying") καὶ αἰτούμενοι ("asking")
>> ἵνα πληρωθῆτε τὴν ἐπίγνωσιν τοῦ θελήματος αὐτοῦ ἐν πάσῃ σοφίᾳ καὶ συνέσει πνευματικῇ

> we have not ceased to pray for you,
>> asking
>> that you may be filled with the knowledge
>> of his will in all spiritual wisdom and
>> understanding (ESV)

Additional Modifiers

Once you have subdivided a text into main clauses and subordinate clauses, the next step would be to line up any modifiers under or above their antecedents. Some parts of speech get further indented. Relative clauses (i.e., clauses that begin with a relative pronoun), for example, are typically indented relative to their antecedent, as in Galatians 3:1:

> Ὦ ἀνόητοι Γαλάται, τίς ὑμᾶς ἐβάσκανεν,
> > οἷς κατ' ὀφθαλμοὺς Ἰησοῦς Χριστὸς
> > προεγράφη ἐσταυρωμένος;
> You foolish Galatians! Who has bewitched you?
> > Before your eyes very Jesus Christ
> > was clearly portrayed as crucified.

Prepositional phrases (phrases that begin with a preposition) can also be indented. Returning to Romans 5:1:

> Δικαιωθέντες οὖν
> > ἐκ πίστεως
> εἰρήνην ἔχομεν πρὸς τὸν θεὸν
> > διὰ τοῦ κυρίου ἡμῶν Ἰησοῦ Χριστοῦ
> Therefore, having been justified
> > by faith
> we have peace with God
> > through our Lord Jesus Christ. (NASB)

The main thought is that believers have peace with God. This peace has come about because of being justified by faith, which is ultimately through the work of the Lord Jesus Christ. Sometimes, however, it might prove best to leave the prepositional phrase connected to the independent clause if it helps indicate more clearly the independent clause. Hence, in John 3:17, rather than:

οὐ γὰρ ἀπέστειλεν ὁ θεὸς τὸν υἱὸν
        εἰς τὸν κόσμον
        ἵνα κρίνῃ τὸν κόσμον,
    ἀλλ' ἵνα σωθῇ ὁ κόσμος δι' αὐτοῦ,

it might prove more helpful to outline the verse as:

οὐ γὰρ ἀπέστειλεν ὁ θεὸς τὸν υἱὸν εἰς τὸν κόσμον
        ἵνα κρίνῃ τὸν κόσμον,
    ἀλλ' ἵνα σωθῇ ὁ κόσμος δι' αὐτοῦ
For God did not send his Son into the world
                to condemn the world,
                but to save the world through him

The main idea is that God did not send his Son into the world
for judgment but for salvation. Similarly, Colossians 1:9 could
be further subdivided as:

οὐ παυόμεθα
    ὑπὲρ ὑμῶν
    προσευχόμενοι καὶ αἰτούμενοι
    ἵνα πληρωθῆτε τὴν ἐπίγνωσιν τοῦ θελήματος αὐτοῦ
        ἐν πάσῃ σοφίᾳ καὶ συνέσει πνευματικῇ
we have not ceased to pray
                    for you,
                    asking
                    that you may be filled with
                                the knowledge
                                of his will
                                in all spiritual
                                wisdom and
                                understanding
                                (ESV)

The main thought of this verse is that Paul has not stopped praying on behalf of the Colossian church. In his unbroken intercession for them he has not stopped asking God to fill them with the knowledge of his will in all spiritual wisdom.

These are examples of how to outline small texts, but what about a longer prose passage? How can you find the main thoughts in a passage that's longer than a verse? Take, for instance, Paul's opening in his letter to the Philippians. What are his main thoughts in those nine verses?

Philippians 1:3–11

3 Εὐχαριστῶ τῷ θεῷ μου

   ἐπὶ πάσῃ τῇ μνείᾳ ὑμῶν

   4 πάντοτε ἐν πάσῃ δεήσει μου

         ὑπὲρ πάντων ὑμῶν,

         μετὰ χαρᾶς τὴν δέησιν ποιούμενος,

   5 ἐπὶ τῇ κοινωνίᾳ ὑμῶν

         εἰς τὸ εὐαγγέλιον

         ἀπὸ τῆς πρώτης ἡμέρας ἄχρι τοῦ νῦν,

   6 πεποιθὼς αὐτὸ τοῦτο

         ὅτι ὁ ἐναρξάμενος ἐν ὑμῖν ἔργον ἀγαθὸν ἐπιτελέσει

            ἄχρι ἡμέρας Χριστοῦ Ἰησοῦ·

7 καθώς ἐστιν δίκαιον ἐμοὶ τοῦτο φρονεῖν

         ὑπὲρ πάντων ὑμῶν,

  διὰ τὸ ἔχειν με

   ἐν τῇ καρδίᾳ ὑμᾶς,

ἔν τε τοῖς δεσμοῖς μου καὶ ἐν τῇ
ἀπολογίᾳ καὶ βεβαιώσει τοῦ εὐαγγελίου
συγκοινωνούς μου τῆς χάριτος πάντας
ὑμᾶς ὄντας·

[8] μάρτυς γάρ μου ὁ θεός,

ὡς ἐπιποθῶ πάντας ὑμᾶς

ἐν σπλάγχνοις Χριστοῦ Ἰησοῦ.

[9] καὶ τοῦτο προσεύχομαι

ἵνα ἡ ἀγάπη ὑμῶν ἔτι μᾶλλον καὶ μᾶλλον
περισσεύῃ

ἐν ἐπιγνώσει καὶ πάσῃ αἰσθήσει,

[10] εἰς τὸ δοκιμάζειν ὑμᾶς τὰ
διαφέροντα,

ἵνα ἦτε εἰλικρινεῖς καὶ ἀπρόσκοποι

εἰς ἡμέραν Χριστοῦ,

[11] πεπληρωμένοι καρπὸν δικαιοσύνης τὸν
διὰ Ἰησοῦ Χριστοῦ

εἰς δόξαν καὶ ἔπαινον θεοῦ.

[3] I thank my God

every time I remember you.

[4] In all my prayers

for all of you,

I always pray with joy

[5] because of your partnership

in the gospel

from the first day until now,

[6] being confident of this,

> that he who began a good work in you will
> carry it on to completion

>> until the day of Christ Jesus.

[7] It is right for me to feel this way

> about all of you,

since I have you in my heart and,

> whether I am in chains or

> defending and confirming the gospel,

> all of you share in God's grace with me.

[8] God can testify

> how I long for all of you

> with the affection of Christ Jesus.

[9] And this is my prayer:

>> that your love may abound more and
>> more

>>> in knowledge and depth of insight,

>>> [10] so that you may be able to discern
>>> what is best

>>> and may be pure and blameless

>>>> for the day of Christ,

>>> [11] filled with the fruit of righteousness
>>> that comes through Jesus Christ—

>>>> to the glory and praise of God.

As you can see, there are two independent clauses in this passage: Paul's giving thanks (v. 3) and his declaration of prayer (v. 9a). If you were to preach Philippians 1:3–11, these two independent clauses would form the main points of the sermon. The indented portions modify each of the respective main clauses. The verses pertaining to Paul's first main point (i.e., vv. 4–8) describe how and why he gives thanks the way he does. The verses pertaining to the second main point (vv. 9b–11) detail the content of Paul's prayer for the Philippians. Besides a two-point (per independent clause) homily, each independent clause and its attending dependent clauses could also comprise its own message if you wanted to spend more time preaching through Philippians, with the dependent clauses representing the main points of the sermon.

Sometimes a sermon text might only have one independent clause. This is the case in Paul's second prayer for the Ephesian church. His prayer in Ephesians 3:14–19 consists of six verses with twelve verbal forms, but only one finite verb outside of a ἵνα clause that governs the whole passage: verse 14, κάμπτω τὰ γόνατά μου πρὸς τὸν πατέρα ("I kneel before the Father").

Paul bows his knees to the Father—a representational way of describing his intercession for the church. The rest of the passage simply unpacks what his prayer entails according to all of the subordinate clauses in vv. 16, 17, 18, and 19. This passage could be preached as a one-point sermon with several subpoints. You could also form the homiletical outline differently: each subpoint could constitute a main point, that is, the characteristics of Paul's intercessory prayer.

OUTLINING NEW TESTAMENT NARRATIVE

While the value of outlining prose is readily apparent, this is not always the case when it comes to narrative passages. Narrative entails the author recounting certain events, and good story-telling involves the deployment of verbs, most often finite verbs, in order to drive the story along. Therefore, finite verbs occur much more frequently in narrative texts than in prose, which means that in any given narrative passage most verses would be left-justified.

Greek scholar Dana Harris offers a different way to map a narrative text. In addition to the outlining principles described above, you have to pay attention to verb tense, characters, dialogue, and actions.[8] One way of keeping track of dialogue would be to indent it under the appropriate verb. Harris writes, "The goal of a narrative outline is to follow the events, people, places, and dialogue in a narrative passage. This will help you to 'tell the story' of the narrative more clearly when you are preaching or teaching through such a passage."[9] Let's consider two examples, Mark 16:1–8 and Matthew 1:18–25.

Mark 16:1–8

In Mark 16:1–8, the independent clauses that drive the action of the passage are: the women bought spices (v. 1), they went to the tomb (v. 2), they questioned each other (v. 3), they beheld the stone (v. 4), they saw a young man (v. 5), they were alarmed (v. 5) and fled from the tomb (v. 8), and they said nothing to

---

8. Dana Harris, *An Introduction to Biblical Greek Grammar: Elementary Syntax and Linguistics* (Grand Rapids: Zondervan, 2020), 441–42. Cf. Robert Chisholm, *From Exegesis to Exposition: A Practical Guide to Using Biblical Hebrew* (Grand Rapids: Baker, 1998), 151–69, who unpacks these "basic ingredients" of stories for Old Testament narratives.

9. Harris, *Greek Grammar*, 442.

anyone (v. 8). You would write these main clauses at the left margin; the other parts of each verse would be indented to varying degrees. The outline of Mark 16 reveals that the passage revolves around the two women, on the one hand: it details their actions and their dialogue before and after their visit to the tomb. On the other hand, the words of the angel comprise a significant amount of the story—almost half, according to the word count in Greek.

Another way of mapping a narrative text is by subdividing the passage into the five basic elements of a story: the introduction, the rising action/conflict between characters, the climax, the falling action (invariably following the climax), and the conclusion or resolution of the conflict.[10] The introduction offers the information necessary to understand the story: to help the reader understand the characters and/or events that take place therein. The introduction might simply describe the occasion or perhaps the setting (spatial, temporal, social) of the story. In the rising action section, the plot of the story develops, introducing and leading the audience to the central conflict, which serves to increase the story's tension. Then comes the climax, which represents the highest level of tension in the narrative, and which serves as the story's fulcrum whereby the tension begins to decrease. This falling action leads finally to the conclusion or resolution of the key conflict. Applying this strategy to Mark 16 yields the following observations:

- Introduction: The women gather after the Sabbath to prepare Jesus's body for burial.

---

10. See Michael Gorman, *Elements of Biblical Exegesis: A Basic Guide for Students and Ministers*, 3rd ed. (Grand Rapids: Baker Academic, 2020), 102, and Jeannine Brown, *The Gospels as Stories* (Grand Rapids: Baker Academic, 2020), 23–42, especially.

- Rising action: On their way to the tomb, they discuss the issue of rolling away the stone.

- Climax: The women encounter the angel who tells them that the tomb is empty because Jesus has been raised from the dead, and that they are to share this news with the disciples.

- Falling action and conclusion: The fearful women flee the tomb and say nothing to anyone.

In either approach, the words of the angel are of paramount importance to the story, and hence they must also be central to the sermon. Furthermore, while the women might be the principal figures in the story, their chief function is to highlight the impossibility of the situation: a corpse to prepare for burial and a huge stone to roll away, on the one hand; and their failed response to the news of Jesus's resurrection, on the other. A sermon based on Mark 16, then, would focus on the message of the resurrection of Jesus, with the details serving to elevate this message.

Matthew 1:18–25

In Matthew 1:18–25, the independent clauses that drive the action of the passage are: Mary is found to be pregnant (v. 18), Joseph wants to divorce her (v. 19), an angel of the Lord appears to him (v. 20), this all took place (v. 22), Joseph did as the angel commanded him (v. 24), he took Mary as his wife (v. 24), he didn't have sexual relations with her (v. 25), he gave the child the name of Jesus (v. 25). Again, you would write these main clauses at the left margin, with the other parts of each verse indented to varying degrees. Thus, from the outline, the actions that drive this passage are: Mary became pregnant through the Holy Spirit; Joseph planned to divorce her because of the pregnancy, but an angel told him not to, explaining the special situation to him, as predicted in Scripture. Consequently, Joseph obeyed the angel, took Mary as his wife, maintained her virginity, and named the child Jesus.

Applying the strategy of the five basic elements of a story yields the following observations:

- Introduction: The statement of purpose of the account: it presents the details of Jesus's birth.

- Rising action: Mary becomes pregnant, and Joseph seeks to divorce her.

- Climax: An angel of the Lord appears to Joseph and explains the unique situation to him, which fulfilled Scripture.

- Falling action and conclusion: Joseph obeys the angel's words, Mary gives birth, and they name the baby Jesus.

Both approaches to this passage, then, generate the same exegetical judgments: the central thrust of the paragraph is the angel's (and Scripture's) words about Jesus's birth and Joseph's obedience to them. Thus, the corresponding sermon should convey this same authorial focus.

OUTLINING OLD TESTAMENT NARRATIVE

You can approach an Old Testament story, like New Testament narrative, using the outlining principles of main and subordinate clauses. However, as Grant Osborne notes, "The first thing we notice about [Old Testament passages] is the lack of subordinate clauses. Diagramming the Old Testament is not nearly as helpful as it is in the New Testament because Hebrew does not employ as many conjunctions."[11] Hebrew scholars recognize that the framework for Hebrew narratives consists of the *waw*-consecutive + the prefixed verb (the "imperfect") + subject.[12] For example, the framework of God creating in Genesis 1 is depicted through a series of *waw*-consecutive-prefixed verb constructions, typified in the first creation day:

> And God said (ויאמר), 'Let there be light,' and there was (ויהי) light. And God saw (וירא) that the light was good. And God separated (ויבדל) the light from the darkness. God called (ויקרא) the light Day, and the darkness he called Night. And there was (ויהי) evening and there was morning, the first day. (Gen 1:3–5)

Other features like character, dialogue, and actions readily come into play. Old Testament scholar Robert Chisholm lists additional narrative elements to pay attention to like repetition and contrast.[13] Kaiser points out how arrangement and selection of material plays a central role in exegesis:

> It becomes critically important to recognize the larger context in which the narrative fits and to ask why the writer used the specific selection of events in the precise sequence in which he placed them. The twin clues to meaning now will be arrangement of episodes and selection of detail.[14]

---

11. Grant Osborne, *The Hermeneutical Spiral: A Comprehensive Introduction to Biblical Interpretation*, 2nd ed. (Downers Grove, IL: IVP, 2006), 51.

12. Cf. Chisholm, *Exegesis to Exposition*, 119–20. This structure is also referred to as the *wayyiqtol* pattern.

13. See Chisholm, *Exegesis to Exposition*, 151–67.

14. Walter Kaiser, *Toward an Exegetical Theology: Biblical Exegesis for Preaching and Teaching* (Grand Rapids: Baker, 1981), 205. Similarly, Chisholm (*Exegesis to Exposition*,

Genesis 18:17–33

The main clauses in the text give us insight into the story. We could summarize their movement like this:

- The Lord affirms his promise of blessing to Abraham and reveals to him his plan to execute judgment against Sodom and Gomorrah.

- Two of the messengers go to Sodom while Abraham remains standing before the Lord.

- Abraham barters with God over the number of righteous people it would take to save the city from divine judgment.

- After he reaches the number ten, the Lord leaves Abraham, who returns to his place.

Most of the words in the narrative come by way of dialogue. Approximately 75 percent of the passage is dialogue; and of this, the Lord and Abraham speak roughly the same number of words in their encounter.

Thus, the account begins with a reiteration of God's promise of blessing and nationhood to Abraham: God will faithfully fulfill his promise to the patriarch. In stark contrast to God's blessing upon Abraham stands the threat of destruction for Sodom and Gomorrah, for whom Abraham boldly intercedes for mercy. In response to the patriarch's plea, God promises conditional mercy: he will spare the cities if there are ten righteous people living in them. The sevenfold repetition of "righteous" and the fourfold mention of "destroy" suggests that God's harsh judgments against sin stem from his righteous nature.

---

151) writes that exegetes must show how the narrative fits into its wider literary context.

Subdividing the passage into the five basic elements of a story would lead us to extend the scope of the passage into the next chapter:

- Introduction: The first half of chapter 18 serves as the introduction to the second half: The three visitors meet Abraham and proclaim to him the news that Sarah will finally bear him a son in one year's time.

- Rising action: The entire passage in reality comprises part of the development of the conflict, which further heightens in chapter 19.

- Climax: God rains down burning sulfur on the cities, but Lot escapes with his two daughters (Gen 19:16–26).

- Falling action and conclusion: Because God remembered his earlier promise to Abraham, he spares Lot's life (Gen 19:27–29).

Overall, what seems most important here is God's faithfulness to the promise he made to Abraham. God ultimately spares Lot not simply because of the patriarch's premeditated pleas but because of the Lord's unconditional promise to Abraham, which includes the idea of nations—like the nation that will come from Lot—being blessed through Abraham.

Interestingly, these two approaches to the story produce different outlines of the passage: the former outline gets absorbed into the introduction and rising-action sections of the latter. This leads to slightly different but complementary emphases from the text. In the first approach, we see that God can deal faithfully with Abraham, while still maintaining his righteous standard in dealing with sin. The second highlights how

God begins to faithfully keep his promise to Abraham to bless other nations through him, by sparing Lot from destruction. In preaching from this passage, then, the sermon should carry this same kind of thrust of God's faithfulness to his people.

Genesis 12:10-20

The main thoughts of this story are:

- Abram goes to Egypt during a time of famine (three times the story mentions him entering Egypt).

- He asks Sarai to lie about their relationship in order to protect him from the Egyptians.

- Pharaoh takes Sarai as his wife and therefore treats Abram well.

- God strikes Pharaoh with plagues for taking Sarai (a point repeated six times in the text).

- Pharaoh gives Sarai back to Abram along with all of his possessions and sends them on their way.

In terms of the five basic elements of a story:

- Introduction: Abram and Sarai go to Egypt because of a famine.

- Rising action: He tells her to lie about their relationship while there, so Pharaoh then takes her as his wife.

- Climax: God pours out plagues on Pharaoh, who as a result confronts Abram about the true nature of his relationship to Sarai.

- Falling action and conclusion: Pharaoh sends the couple on their way with all of their possessions.

The story offers the reader a picture of how God fulfills his promise to Abraham in Genesis 12:1–3: God increases his possessions through Pharaoh ("I will bless you and make your name great"), and God curses Pharaoh for taking away Sarai ("him who dishonors you I will curse"). Once again, a sermon on this text should highlight God's faithfulness to his promise to Abraham and the sovereign outworking of his plans.

THE ROLE OF CHIASMUS IN OUTLINING

Biblical authors are fond of deploying chiasmus in their writings. Chiasmus (or chiasm) is a rhetorical structure that revolves around parallels and inversion, whereby the inverted section constitutes the central point of the text, depicted in its simplest form by the structure:

A

  B

A'

The main point B is bracketed by the parallel lines A and A' ("A Prime"). Because the biblical authors lived in a primarily oral and not written environment, rhetorical features like chiasmus would have been readily recognized by the audience because they help the listener mentally structure a teaching or story so as to remember it and to be better able to share it with others.[15] This is actually quite similar to what we find with many good homilies today. While Western preachers do not deploy chiasmus, we do offer other means of facilitating understanding, remembering, and reproduction: We preach

---

15. H. Van Dyke Parunak ("Some Axioms for Literary Architecture," *Semitics* 8 [1982]: 2) notes how, in contrast to modern literature, biblical writings are "essentially aural and intended to be understood with the ear, and not with the eye."

only a few main points (rather than say, ten); sometimes these points are announced near the beginning of the message, giving the congregation mental pockets to fill up with sermon content. The sermon points are syntactically parallel (rather than dissimilar) and flow from one to the next (rather than being disjointed); and they are structured simply and sometimes alliteratively (e.g., main points might begin with the same letter of the alphabet).

As noted, the basic chiastic structure follows an A-B-A' pattern, whereby A and A' are linguistically and/or thematically parallel, and B is the unique subunit and the centerpiece of the chiasm. Chiasmus often appears in poetry like the Psalms. Thus, for example, Psalm 51:17:

> A   The sacrifices of God
>
>> B   are a broken spirit;
>>
>> B'   a broken and contrite heart,
>
> A'   O God, you will not despise.

The focal point of the verse is the B/B' subunit: the lowly state of the believer. Chiasmus can consist of a single verse, or it can span large swathes of text.[16] If you believe a chiasm might be present in a passage, the final determination must be made from the original languages and not from a translation. Academic commentaries can be extremely helpful for detecting chiasmus.

So then, how would chiasmus factor into the outlining of a passage?

---

16. In his Romans commentary, Doug Moo, for example, identifies a lengthy chiasmus stretching from Romans 5 to Romans 8.

Matthew 2:1–12

I noted in chapter 2 that the story of the magi constitutes a complete unit of thought. One thing that English translations cannot convey is the chiastic structure of the pericope, as laid out below.

> ¹ Now after Jesus was born in Bethlehem (ἐν Βηθλέεμ) of Judea in the days of Herod (Ἡρώδου) the king, behold, wise men from the east came to Jerusalem, ² saying,
>
>> "Where is he who has been born king (βασιλεὺς) of the Jews? For we saw his star when it rose (ἀστέρα ἐν τῇ ἀνατολῇ) and have come to worship him (προσκυνῆσαι αὐτῷ)."
>>
>>> ³ When Herod (Ἡρώδης) the king heard this, he was troubled, and all Jerusalem with him; ⁴ and assembling all the chief priests and scribes (συναγαγὼν πάντας τοὺς ἀρχιερεῖς καὶ γραμματεῖς) of the people, he inquired (ἐπυνθάνετο) of them where the Christ (ὁ χριστὸς) was to be born. ⁵ They told him, "In Bethlehem of Judea, for so it is written by the prophet:
>>>
>>>> ⁶ "'And you, O Bethlehem, in the land of Judah, are by no means least among the rulers of Judah; for from you shall come a ruler who will shepherd my people Israel.'"
>>>
>>> ⁷ Then Herod (Ἡρώδης) summoned the wise men (καλέσας τοὺς μάγους) secretly and ascertained from them what time the star had appeared. ⁸ And he sent them to Bethlehem, saying, "Go and search (ἐξετάσατε) diligently for the child (τοῦ παιδίου), and when you have found him, bring me word, that I too may come and worship him."

⁹ After listening to the king (βασιλέως), they went on their way. And behold, the star that they had seen when it rose (ἀστὴρ ὃν εἶδον ἐν τῇ ἀνατολῇ) went before them until it came to rest over the place where the child was. ¹⁰ When they saw the star, they rejoiced exceedingly with great joy. ¹¹ And going into the house, they saw the child with Mary his mother, and they fell down and worshiped him (προσεκύνησαν αὐτῷ). Then, opening their treasures, they offered him gifts, gold and frankincense and myrrh.

¹² And being warned in a dream not to return to Herod (Ἡρῴδην), they departed to their own country (εἰς τὴν χώραν) by another way. (ESV)

The story is structured around an A-B-C-D-C'-B'-A' linguistic chiasm, with the parallel units:

A in Bethlehem (ἐν Βηθλέεμ) ... Herod (Ἡρῴδου)

    B king (βασιλεὺς) ... star when it rose (ἀστέρα ἐν τῇ ἀνατολῇ) ... worship him (προσκυνῆσαι αὐτῷ).

        C Herod (Ἡρῴδης) ... assembling all the chief priests and scribes (συναγαγὼν πάντας τοὺς ἀρχιερεῖς καὶ γραμματεῖς) ... he inquired (ἐπυνθάνετο) ... the Christ (ὁ χριστὸς)

            D "And you, O Bethlehem, in the land of Judah, are by no means least among the rulers of Judah; for from you shall come a ruler who will shepherd my people Israel."

        C' Herod (Ἡρῴδης) summoned the wise men (καλέσας τοὺς μάγους) ... "Go and search (ἐξετάσατε) ... the child (τοῦ παιδίου)

    B' king (βασιλέως) ... the star that they had seen when it rose (ἀστὴρ ὃν εἶδον ἐν τῇ ἀνατολῇ) ... worshiped him (προσεκύνησαν αὐτῷ).

A' Herod (Ἡρῴδην) ... to their own country (εἰς τὴν χώραν)

Based on its chiastic structure, the climax of this passage is Scripture's declaration about the birth of Jesus, which affirms his Davidic lineage and his divine appointment to rule over Israel as the nation's messianic Shepherd. Therefore, in preaching this story, that ought to be the central thrust of the sermon: the prophetic declaration of Jesus's messiahship.

Galatians 4:1–7

Having described how the coming of Christ spells an end to the authority of the Mosaic law in the life of the believer, Paul begins to discuss the nature of our sonship in Christ in Galatians 4:1–7, a pericope built around a chiasm:

> [1] What I am saying is that as long as an heir is underage (ὁ κληρονόμος νήπιός ἐστιν), he is no different from a slave (οὐδὲν διαφέρει δούλου), although he owns the whole estate.

>> [2] The heir is subject to guardians and trustees until the time set by his father (τοῦ πατρός). [3] So also, when we were underage (ἤμεν νήπιοι), we were in slavery under the elemental spiritual forces of the world. [4] But when the set time had fully come, God sent his Son (ἐξαπέστειλεν ὁ θεὸς τὸν υἱὸν αὐτοῦ),

>>> born of a woman, born under the law,

>>> [5] to redeem those under the law, that we might receive adoption to sonship.

>> [6] Because you are his sons (ἐστε υἱοί), God sent the Spirit of his Son (ἐξαπέστειλεν ὁ θεὸς τὸ πνεῦμα τοῦ υἱοῦ αὐτοῦ) into our hearts, the Spirit who calls out, "Abba, Father" (Αββα ὁ πατήρ).

> [7] So you are no longer a slave, but God's child (οὐκέτι εἶ δοῦλος ἀλλὰ υἱός); and since you are his child, God has made you also an heir (κληρονόμος).

The A-B-C-B'-A' structure involves the parallel units:

> A the heir is underage (ὁ κληρονόμος νήπιός ἐστιν) ... no different from a slave (οὐδὲν διαφέρει δούλου)

> > B father (τοῦ πατρός) ... we are underage (ἤμεν νήπιοι) ... God sent his Son (ἐξαπέστειλεν ὁ θεὸς τὸν υἱὸν αὐτοῦ),

> > > C born of a woman, born under the law, to redeem those under the law, that we might receive adoption to sonship.

> > B' you are his sons (ἐστε υἱοί), God sent the Spirit of his Son (ἐξαπέστειλεν ὁ θεὸς τὸ πνεῦμα τοῦ υἱοῦ αὐτοῦ) ... "Abba, Father" (Αββα ὁ πατήρ)

> A' you are no longer a slave, but God's child (οὐκέτι εἶ δοῦλος ἀλλὰ υἱός) ... God made you an heir (κληρονόμος).

In his argumentation against the invasive false teaching that the Galatians must put on the yoke of the Mosaic law, Paul says here that God always had an appointed time when the law would no longer have jurisdiction over his people. The chiastic structure of Galatians 4:1–7 reveals that the climax to Paul's thought is v. 5: in the incarnation, Christ came under the law to redeem his people from the law to grant them divine sonship. That should be the thrust of a sermon on this passage, as well. Further, each pair of verses in the chiasm could constitute a main point in the homily. That is, the A-A' verse pairing could form one main point and the B-B' pair could form a second. For example, if the main point is that in the incarnation God has made us his children, then the following points would unpack that idea:

Because of the incarnation we've been transferred from being a slave of sin to God's child.

Because of the incarnation we've been transformed from being enslaved to the spiritual forces of the world to intimacy with God through his Spirit.

CONCLUSION

Some preachers bristle at the thought of being so rigidly tied to a text's structure. After all, the text has to be able to preach! Some might object: Doesn't all this attention to outlining stunt the preacher's ability to preach the biblical text in an unfettered and engaging way? Yes and no.

Yes, in this sense: To preach the biblical text faithfully means faithfully following the thrusts and nuances of that text. The text makes the preacher; the preacher does not make the text. Sometimes we need reminding of that. The biblical text must never be subject to the preacher's personal whims. If a passage does not say what the preacher wants it to say or does not say it in quite the way the preacher would like it said, then move on: find another text, or better yet, preach a topical or textual-topical sermon. Do not force the text to parrot personal preferences. So, yes, the sermon is absolutely constrained by the text.

But on the other hand, no it is not. In her Greek grammar, Dana Harris offers the helpful analogy of a jazz musician.[17] Excellent jazz musicians have spent countless hours learning the fundamentals of music theory as well as practicing various musical scales. In fact, much of this learning is standardized according to the instrument. All guitarists, for example, learn the same guitar theory, the same scales, and so on. Yet no two guitarists sound exactly alike. Harris writes:

---

17. Harris, *Greek Grammar*, 435–36.

Analogously, a biblical text has a certain structure that is determined by the syntax used in that text, like a musical composition. This basic structure is understood by identifying the basic syntactic units and how they function. … Once the structure is understood, however, there are any number of ways that the text can be faithfully exposited. Knowing the basic structure of a given biblical text actually gives the Spirit-led freedom to proclaim the same texts in a variety of ways depending on the context and the needs of the audience. So knowing a text's structure actually leads to more freedom to exposit the text.[18]

The sermon must move in the direction of the biblical passage. There is rhetorical and pastoral freedom along the way—this is especially true when it comes, for example, to preaching narratives. After all, while the biblical authors fully expected their texts to be heard, read, and used to instruct the community, they did not write their texts with an eye to future sermon-writing ventures. Therefore, there is a fair measure of rhetorical and pastoral freedom for us as preachers. Nevertheless, the message must always travel along the same path as the sacred text.

Having mapped the text in this way, you are well on the way to the homiletical outline, from which springs forth the sermon notes or manuscript. But one more small but significant step remains, and it is to this step we now turn.

RESOURCES

Chisholm, R. *From Exegesis to Exposition: A Practical Guide to Using Biblical Hebrew*. Grand Rapids: Baker, 1998.

---

18. Harris, *Greek Grammar*, 436.

Duvall, J., and J. Hays. *Grasping God's Word: A Hands-On Approach to Reading, Interpreting, and Applying the Bible.* 3rd ed. Grand Rapids: Zondervan, 2012.

Fee, G. *New Testament Exegesis: A Handbook for Students and Pastors.* 3rd ed. Louisville: Westminster John Knox, 2002.

Gorman, M. *Elements of Biblical Exegesis: A Basic Guide for Students and Ministers.* 3rd ed. Grand Rapids: Baker Academic, 2020.

Greidanus, S. *The Modern Preacher and the Ancient Text: Interpreting and Preaching Biblical Literature.* Grand Rapids: Eerdmans, 1989.

Guthrie, G., and J. Duvall. *Biblical Greek Exegesis: A Graded Approach to Learning Intermediate and Advanced Greek.* Grand Rapids: Zondervan, 1998.

Huffman, D. *The Handy Guide to New Testament Greek: Grammar, Syntax, and Diagramming.* Grand Rapids: Kregel Academic, 2012.

Kaiser, W. *Toward an Exegetical Theology: Biblical Exegesis for Preaching and Teaching.* Grand Rapids: Baker, 1981.

Köstenberger, A., B. Merkle, and R. Plummer. *Going Deeper with New Testament Greek: An Intermediate Study of the Grammar and Syntax of the New Testament.* Nashville: B&H Academic, 2016.

Liefeld, W. *New Testament Exposition: From Text to Sermon.* Grand Rapids: Zondervan, 1989.

Longman III, T. "Literary Approaches to Biblical Interpretation." In *Foundations of Contemporary Interpretation: Six Volumes in One.* Edited by M. Silva. Grand Rapids: Zondervan, 1987.

Mounce, W. *A Graded Reader of Biblical Greek.* Grand Rapids: Zondervan, 1996.

Osborne, G. *The Hermeneutical Spiral: A Comprehensive Introduction to Biblical Interpretation.* 2nd ed. Downers Grove, IL: IVP Academic, 2006.

Schreiner, T. *Interpreting the Pauline Epistles.* 2nd ed. Grand Rapids: Baker, 2011.

Sowell, E. *An Intermediate Guide to Greek Diagramming.* KoineWorks Diagramming. Lexel Software, LLC, 2002.

CHAPTER 5

THE OUTLINE BEFORE
THE OUTLINE

FROM PASSAGE OUTLINE TO
EXEGETICAL SUMMARY OUTLINE

WHEN OUR THREE KIDS were young, I recall many a road trip where invariably at least one of them would ask that proverbial question, "Are we there yet?" Often this was followed by, "How much longer?" You've chosen your sermon passage, determining the proper upper and lower limits of your text. You've read it in light of its co-text. Further, you've syntactically mapped your passage, leaving you with a series of independent and subordinate clauses. The latter step has perhaps left you wanting to get to that all-important sermon outline. You are almost there, but not quite. Before the homiletical outline can be written, you should write an exegetical *summary* outline (emphasis on "summary")—a kind of "pre-homiletical" outline—based solely on the exegetical outline. The purpose of the summary outline is to help you capture the flow and movement of the argument or of the story by identifying and grouping together the subunits of the passage. Skipping or ignoring this small but important step can lead to a confusing sermon outline. Key to this stage is writing out only the independent clauses, which drive the action of the text.

GALATIANS 1:11–24

Exegetical Outline

In verses 11–12, the main clause is Γνωρίζω γὰρ ὑμῖν, ἀδελφοί, τὸ εὐαγγέλιον τὸ εὐαγγελισθὲν ὑπ' ἐμοῦ ὅτι οὐκ ἔστιν κατὰ ἄνθρωπον ("I want you to know, brothers and sisters, that the gospel I preached is not of human origin").[1] In the main clauses of verses 13–14, Paul describes his religious past: Ἠκούσατε γὰρ τὴν ἐμὴν ἀναστροφήν ("For you have heard of my previous way of life"), followed by the main, καὶ προέκοπτον ἐν τῷ Ἰουδαϊσμῷ ("I was advancing in Judaism"). After his encounter with Christ, he first describes what he did not do: εὐθέως οὐ προσανεθέμην σαρκὶ καὶ αἵματι ("my immediate response was not to consult any human being"), followed by his geographical movement using main clauses in verses 17–21: οὐδὲ ἀνῆλθον εἰς Ἱεροσόλυμα ("I did not go up to Jerusalem"), ἀλλὰ ἀπῆλθον εἰς Ἀραβίαν ("but I went into Arabia"), ἀνῆλθον εἰς Ἱεροσόλυμα ("I went up to Jerusalem"), ἕτερον δὲ τῶν ἀποστόλων οὐκ εἶδον ("I saw none of the other apostles"), ἦλθον εἰς τὰ κλίματα τῆς Συρίας καὶ τῆς Κιλικίας ("Then I went to Syria and Cilicia"). Paul finishes of his story by describing the church's response to his newfound faith using main clauses: ἤμην δὲ ἀγνοούμενος ("I was personally

---

1. Recall, ὅτι clauses, while syntactically subordinate, can sometimes fill out the main thought in the independent clause, thereby functioning like part of the main clause. See the discussion of the ὅτι clause in the section, "Dependent Clauses" in chapter four above.

unknown"), μόνον δὲ ἀκούοντες ἦσαν ("they only heard"), καὶ
ἐδόξαζον ἐν ἐμοὶ τὸν θεόν ("and they praised God because of me").
Translated into English, the outline looks like this:

> [11] I want you to know, brothers and sisters,
>
>> that the gospel I preached
>>
>>> is not of human origin.
>>>
>>> [12] I did not receive it
>>>
>>>> from any man,
>>>
>>> nor was I taught it;
>>>
>>> rather, I received it by revelation from Jesus
>>> Christ.
>
> [13] For you have heard of my previous way of life in
> Judaism,
>
>> how intensely I persecuted the church of God and
>> tried to destroy it.
>
> [14] I was advancing
>
>> in Judaism
>>
>> beyond many of my own age among my people
>>
>> and was extremely zealous for the traditions of
>> my fathers.
>
>> [15] But when God, who set me apart
>>
>>> from my mother's womb and called me
>>>
>>>> by his grace, was pleased
>>>
>>> [16] to reveal his Son in me so that I might
>>> preach him
>>>
>>>> among the Gentiles,

my immediate response was not to consult any human being.

[17] I did not go up

    to Jerusalem to see those who were apostles

        before I was,

but I went

    into Arabia. Later I returned

        to Damascus.

[18] Then after three years,

I went up

    to Jerusalem to get acquainted with Cephas and stayed with him fifteen days.

[19] I saw none of the other apostles

    —only James, the Lord's brother.

    [20] I assure you before God that what I am writing you is no lie.

[21] Then I went

    to Syria and Cilicia.

[22] I was personally unknown to the churches of Judea that are

    in Christ.

[23] They only heard the report:

    "The man who formerly persecuted us is now preaching the faith he once tried to destroy."

[24] And they praised God

    because of me.

Exegetical Summary Outline (of the Independent Clauses)

The exegetical outline identifies the independent and dependent clauses. By themselves, they do not indicate the flow of Paul's thought. The grouping together of the independent clauses facilitates this essential step. The exegetical summary outline should be done in English because it is from your summary outline that your homiletical outline will emerge. The summary outline should correspond to the wording of the passage:

1. Paul wants the church to know that his gospel isn't of human origin but from Christ. (v. 11)

2. The church has heard of his former way of life in Judaism as a persecutor of the church. (v. 13)

3. The church has heard how he was advancing past his Jewish contemporaries. (v. 13)

4. After encountering Jesus, he did not consult with anybody. (vv. 14–24)

   a. He went away to Arabia and returned to Damascus. (v. 17)

   b. He then went to Jerusalem to visit Peter. (v. 18)

   c. He saw none of the other apostles. (v. 19)

   d. He went to the region of Syria and Cilicia. (v. 21)

   e. He was unknown there. (v. 22)

   f. They only heard that the one who persecuted the church is now preaching the faith. (v. 23)

   g. They glorified God on account of Paul. (v. 24)

The first subunit in verses 11–12 deals with the origin and authority of Paul's gospel message. The next subsection (v. 13) describes Paul's former way of life in Judaism. The third paragraph (vv. 14–24) details how Paul lacked contact with other apostles after his conversion, as well as with the churches in Syria and Cilicia, who, because of his about-face in regard to Christianity, praised God on account of him.

Because this is the simplest of the steps involved in the exegetical enterprise, it is easily missed or even skipped. But a simple glance at the summary outline reveals the train of the apostle's thought in Galatians 1:11–24 in a way that the exegetical outline does not. The exegetical outline reveals the different main and subordinate thoughts that comprise the passage. The summary outline gives clarity to Paul's argument and flow of thought. And it is the text's movement that will, in turn, give your sermon its own flow and bring it a crisper coherence.

Homiletical Outline

With Paul's flow of thought in Galatians 1:11–24 mapped, you then convert this summary outline into a homiletical outline. The summary outline is obviously descriptive and essentially repeats the words of the text. Such an outline would never do for a sermon for a couple of reasons. Mere description makes the text seem remote: it's about Paul and those churches. You need to help the audience place themselves in the text. A good sermon outline does that. Also, our job as preachers is to try to preach a text in a way that helps your people remember the teaching of a passage; simply repeating lines from a text does not do much to stimulate memory.

If the entirety of Galatians 1:11–24 comprised the sermon text, then each subunit would constitute a main point in the sermon. One possible homiletical outline would be:

1. The gospel we believe in originates from the risen Jesus himself. (vv. 11–12, 16b–20)

2. The gospel we believe in has the power to radically change a person's life. (vv. 13–16a, 21–24)

The passage is, strictly speaking, about Paul—as the exegetical and summary outlines demonstrate—but the gospel, which changed Paul's life and which he now preaches, applies directly to us.

If, conversely, you decided to preach several sermons from Galatians 1, you would simply use one or two subunits, for example, Galatians 1:11–12:

1. Christians need to recognize that the gospel has a completely divine origin.

   a. It's not worldly in its orientation.

   b. It didn't emerge from human transmission.

   c. It didn't arise from human tradition.

Notice again, the points are more rhetorical in form for the sermon rather than merely historical, descriptive, or character specific—the way they are in the exegetical summary outline.

When moving from the exegetical summary outline to the homiletical outline, it is important to keep in mind that, to cite the old proverb, there is more than one way to skin a cat. In other words, there is more than one way to structure a text homiletically while remaining true to authorial intent. As previously mentioned, when the New Testament authors were composing their texts, they did not see themselves as writing sermons.[2] Doubtless they assumed their story or their letter would be read communally and privately, forming the basis of catechetical instruction and proclamation. But their primary impulse was not to write in such a way as to easily facilitate the crafting of future sermons. Had this been the case, then there probably would have been only one way to structure the biblical text homiletically. But there is not just one way. Therefore, another way you could structure a sermon for Galatians 1:11–24 would be:

1. God is glorified when he radically changes a person's life through the gospel. (vv. 13–16a, 23–24)

2. The work of the gospel in a person's life is confirmed by the rest of the church. (vv. 16b–23)

MATTHEW 1:18-25

Exegetical Outline

Verse 18a begins with a summary statement for this story, but the action of the account begins with the main clause in the rest of the verse: εὑρέθη ἐν γαστρὶ ἔχουσα ("she was found to be pregnant"). The main clause in verse 19 is ἐβουλήθη λάθρα ἀπολῦσαι αὐτήν ("he had in mind to divorce her quietly"), followed by the independent clauses in verses 20, 22, 24, and 25: ἰδοὺ ἄγγελος κυρίου κατ᾽ ὄναρ ἐφάνη αὐτῷ ("an angel of the Lord appeared to him in a dream"), τοῦτο δὲ ὅλον γέγονεν ("all this took place"), ἐποίησεν ὡς προσέταξεν αὐτῷ ὁ ἄγγελος

---

2. Perhaps the exceptions to this phenomenon might be Hebrews, James, and John. See B. Witherington, *Letters and Homilies for Jewish Christians: A Socio-Rhetorical Commentary on Hebrews, James, and Jude* (Downers Grove, IL: IVP Academic, 2007).

κυρίου ("he did what the angel of the Lord commanded") and παρέλαβεν τὴν γυναῖκα αὐτοῦ ("took Mary home as his wife"), οὐκ ἐγίνωσκεν αὐτὴν ("he did not consummate their marriage"), and ἐκάλεσεν τὸ ὄνομα αὐτοῦ Ἰησοῦν ("he gave him the name Jesus"), respectively.

Translated into English, the outline looks like this:

[18] This is how the birth of Jesus the Messiah came about:

> His mother Mary was pledged to be married to Joseph, but before they came together,

she was found to be pregnant through the Holy Spirit.

> [19] Because Joseph her husband was faithful to the law, and yet did not want to expose her to public disgrace,

he had in mind to divorce her quietly.

> [20] But after he had considered this,

an angel of the Lord appeared to him in a dream and said,

> "Joseph son of David, do not be afraid to take Mary home as your wife, because what is conceived in her is from the Holy Spirit. [21] She will give birth to a son, and you are to give him the name Jesus, because he will save his people from their sins."

[22] All this took place

> to fulfill what the Lord had said through the prophet:

> > [23] "The virgin will conceive and give birth to a son, and they will call him Immanuel" (which means "God with us").

[24] When Joseph woke up,

he did

    what the angel of the Lord had commanded him

and took Mary home as his wife.

[25] But he did not consummate their marriage

    until she gave birth to a son.

And he gave him the name Jesus.

Exegetical Summary Outline (of the Independent Clauses)

The mapping of independent and dependent clauses in the Greek exegetical outline does not indicate the flow of Matthew's thought. You need to group the main clauses together to facilitate this step. As before, the summary outline should match the wording of the passage:

1. The account of Jesus's birth. (v. 18a)

2. Mary was pregnant by the Holy Spirit. (v. 18b)

3. Joseph planned to divorce her. (v. 19)

4. This all (Mary's pregnancy) happened according to the word of the Lord through the prophet. (vv. 20–21)

5. Joseph obeyed the angel's words. (v. 24)

   a. He took Mary as his wife. (v. 24)

   b. He refrained from consummating the marriage. (v. 24)

   c. He gave the baby the name Jesus. (v. 25)

In the pericope, the first part of verse 18 offers a summary of the account. The second half of verse 18 plus verse 19 describe Mary's unexpected and miraculous pregnancy and Joseph's response to it. Verses 20–21 relate how Mary's pregnancy is the fulfillment of Isaianic prophecy. Verse 24 describes Joseph's new, obedient course of action, concluding with Joseph giving Jesus his name.

Homiletical Outline

With the story's movement captured, you convert the summary outline into a homiletical outline, again making sure that the points are more rhetorical and exhortative than otherwise done in the exegetical summary outline. Because it represents a narrative account and because it is not long, it would be better for you not to preach just a subunit but rather preach the entire pericope. One way to transform the exegetical summary outline into a sermon outline would be:

1. Sometimes God interrupts our plans with his plans. (vv. 18–19)

2. God desires that we make his plans our plans. (vv. 20–25)

Matthew's story is about the birth of Jesus the Messiah. While this truth is of paramount importance to believers, we still need to help our audience relate the story directly to their lives. This would be one way of doing that. Still, recognizing that there is more than one way to structure a text homiletically, another outline could be:

1. Jesus's birth makes us uncomfortable. (vv. 18–19)

2. Jesus's birth fulfills Scripture. (vv. 22–23)

3. Jesus's birth must lead us to greater obedience. (vv. 24–25)

GENESIS 18:17–33

Exegetical Outline

The main clauses for this story consist of the Lord's rhetorical question about Abraham's future (vv. 17–18), his declaration of Sodom and Gomorrah's sin (vv. 20–21), the departure of the two visitors and Abraham standing before and approaching the Lord to speak to him (vv. 22–23), his back-and-forth dialogue with God (vv. 23–32), followed by the Lord's and Abraham's departures (v. 33).

Translated into English, the outline looks like this:

> [17] The LORD said, "Shall I hide from Abraham what I am about to do,

>> [18] seeing that Abraham shall surely become a great and mighty nation, and all the nations of the earth shall be blessed in him? [19] For I have chosen him, that he may command his children and his household after him to keep the way of the LORD by doing righteousness and justice, so that the LORD may bring to Abraham what he has promised him."

> [20] Then the LORD said,

>> "Because the outcry against Sodom and Gomorrah is great and their sin is very grave, [21] I will go down to see whether they have done altogether according to the outcry that has come to me. And if not, I will know."

> [22] So the men turned from there and went toward Sodom,

> but Abraham still stood before the LORD.

> [23] Then Abraham drew near and said,

"Will you indeed sweep away the righteous with the wicked? [24] Suppose there are fifty righteous within the city. Will you then sweep away the place and not spare it for the fifty righteous who are in it? [25] Far be it from you to do such a thing, to put the righteous to death with the wicked, so that the righteous fare as the wicked! Far be that from you! Shall not the Judge of all the earth do what is just?"

[26] And the LORD said,

"If I find at Sodom fifty righteous in the city, I will spare the whole place for their sake."

[27] Abraham answered and said,

"Behold, I have undertaken to speak to the Lord, I who am but dust and ashes. [28] Suppose five of the fifty righteous are lacking. Will you destroy the whole city for lack of five?"

And he said,

"I will not destroy it if I find forty-five there."

[29] Again he spoke to him and said,

"Suppose forty are found there."

He answered,

"For the sake of forty I will not do it."

[30] Then he said,

"Oh let not the Lord be angry, and I will speak. Suppose thirty are found there."

He answered,

"I will not do it, if I find thirty there."

[31] He said,

> "Behold, I have undertaken to speak to the Lord.
> Suppose twenty are found there."

He answered,

> "For the sake of twenty I will not destroy it."

[32] Then he said,

> "Oh let not the Lord be angry, and I will speak
> again but this once. Suppose ten are found there."

He answered,

> "For the sake of ten I will not destroy it."

[33] And the LORD went his way,

> when he had finished speaking to Abraham,

and Abraham returned to his place.

Exegetical Summary Outline (of the Independent Clauses)

Grouping together the main thoughts of the story yields the
following flow of the passage:

1. God declares that he will not hide what he is about
   to do from Abraham. (v. 17)

2. God speaks to Abraham about Sodom and
   Gomorrah. (v. 20)

3. The visitors departed from the scene, but Abraham
   remained before the Lord. (v. 22)

4. Abraham petitions God for Sodom and Gomorrah.
   (vv. 23–32)

   a. Abraham offers his first petition for Sodom and
      Gomorrah. (v. 23)

    b. Abraham offers his second petition for Sodom and Gomorrah, and God responds. (v. 27)

    c. Abraham offers his third petition for Sodom and Gomorrah, and God responds. (v. 29)

    d. Abraham offers his fourth petition for Sodom and Gomorrah, and God responds. (v. 30)

    e. Abraham offers his fifth petition for Sodom and Gomorrah, and God responds. (v. 31)

    f. Abraham offers his sixth petition for Sodom and Gomorrah, and God responds. (v. 32)

  5. God leaves the scene, and Abraham returns to his place. (v. 33)

The story begins with God reminding Abraham of his unconditional promise to bless him and to bless the nations through him (vv. 17–19). Besides not hiding this from Abraham, neither does he withhold his threat of impending judgment upon Sodom and Gomorrah (vv. 20–21). Verse 22 transitions from God's proclamation of judgment to Abraham's intercessory pleas. The largest section of the account describes Abraham's intercession on behalf of Sodom and Gomorrah (vv. 23–32). In the final verse God and Abraham part ways.

Homiletical Outline

Having traced the movement of the passage, you can use this outline to produce the sermon outline, based on the mapping of the passage. Considering how the wider context of Genesis informs this text (see chapter 3 above), one way to capture and convert the exegetical summary outline for this story would be:

1. Because of God's faithfulness, we can pursue God for the sake of others. (vv. 17–20)

2. Because of God's faithfulness, we can pursue God humbly yet boldly. (vv. 23–32)

3. Because of God's faithfulness, he gets to decide when our pursuit of him is over. (v. 33)

Or perhaps:

1. God's faithful character assures us of the good he has planned for us. (vv. 17–19)

2. God's faithful character enables us to secure an audience with him. (vv. 22b–23a, 33)

3. God's faithful character enables us to bring our concerns before him. (vv. 23b–32)

The biblical author has given us this story to teach us something about God, not Abraham. Any sermon outline of this text should reflect this.

CONCLUSION

The exegetical summary outline enables you to capture the flow of a passage, helping you to organize the text before preaching it, thereby enabling you to produce a more coherent sermon. Sometimes the congregation finds a sermon confusing because it lacks the requisite organization to discern and to trace how the argument or story moves along from beginning to end. Without this intermediate step, the preacher is more likely to offer a confusing homily that pulls in many, sometimes competing, directions, all the while lacking a central thread. Or you might fall into the trap of delivering an overly complicated, twelve-point, hard-to-follow message. This small but significant step in the sermon-writing process helps to prevent these kinds of things from happening.

Having worked through the important matters of structure—both of the co-text and of the passage itself—leading to the exegetical summary outline and the homiletical outline, there still remains the question of the grammatical and syntactical details: the minutiae. How do these micro-elements factor into the sermon? It is to this question that we now turn.

CHAPTER 6

MANAGING THE MINUTIAE

HOW THE TEXT MAKES ITS POINT MATTERS

WE HAVE ALL made broad, sweeping generalizations at one time or another: Quarterbacks are cocky. Baptists are legalistic. Beautiful women are vain. Suburbanites are unfriendly. While the Bible pronounces timeless truths, the biblical authors communicate these truths with different nuances. To preach a biblical passage faithfully, you must not only preach the text with the same exegetical thrust of the biblical author, but your message must try to reflect those same subtleties reflected in the text. The grammatical and syntactical details of the passage reveal the nuances of the author's message.

Two words that are often bandied about the corridors of the biblical language departments of seminaries are "grammar" and "syntax." These do not refer to the same linguistic features, although they do refer to overlapping categories. In this book, "syntax" refers to the bigger elements of a text: sentences, clauses, and phrases, and the interrelationship between these components. As Grant Osborne notes, "Syntax is structural at the core."[1] Conversely, "grammar" refers not to the sentence, clause, or phrase, but to the words that comprise these larger chunks of text.[2] In this chapter we'll begin by examining syntactical nuances, then move to grammatical nuances; and finally, we'll look at semantic analysis (word studies), which is the easiest tool to use but is often misused by preachers. So how do the biblical writers nuance their message?

SYNTACTICAL NUANCES

Recognizing the value of syntax for the task of exegesis, Walter Kaiser writes that "syntax is one of the most important avenues for the interpreter to use in reconstructing the thread of the writer's meaning. The way in which words are put together so as to form phrases, clauses, and sentences will aid us in discovering the author's pattern of meaning."[3] There are several significant ways in which the biblical authors can deploy syntax to create nuance.

Repetition

The easiest way to generate nuance is simply through repetition. Often, the writer will repeat a specific word or a phrase. Genesis describes God's initial call to Abram like this:

---

1. Grant Osborne, *The Hermeneutical Spiral: A Comprehensive Introduction to Biblical Interpretation*, 2nd ed. (Downers Grove, IL: IVP, 2006), 113. So, too, Robert Chisholm (*From Exegesis to Exposition: A Practical Guide to Using Biblical Hebrew* [Grand Rapids: Baker, 1998], 57), who defines "syntax" as "the study of how forms function, interrelate with other forms, and combine to produce sentences."

2. For a helpful discussion of the distinction between grammar and syntax, see Osborne, *Spiral*, 113–14.

3. Walter Kaiser, *Toward an Exegetical Theology: Biblical Exegesis for Preaching and Teaching* (Grand Rapids: Baker, 1981), 89.

> The LORD had said to Abram, "Go from your country, your people and your father's household to the land I will show you. 'I will make you into a great nation, and I will *bless* you; I will make your name great, and you will be a *blessing*. I will *bless* those who *bless* you, and whoever curses you I will curse; and all peoples on earth will be *blessed* through you.'" (Gen 12:1–3 NIV, emphasis added)

The author casts the Abrahamic call using the language of "blessing." At the heart of the Abrahamic covenant, then, is divine blessing: blessing to the patriarch and to the nations through him. Word repetition can be observed in Zechariah 12:10–14 (NIV):

> And I will pour out on the house of David and the inhabitants of Jerusalem a spirit of grace and supplication. They will look on me, the one they have pierced, and they will *mourn* for him as one *mourns* for an only child, and *grieve* bitterly for him as one *grieves* for a first-born son. On that day the *weeping* in Jerusalem will be as great as the *weeping* of Hadad Rimmon in the plain of Megiddo. The land will *mourn*, each clan by itself, with their wives by themselves: the clan of the house of David and their wives, the clan of the house of Nathan and their wives, the clan of the house of Levi and their wives, the clan of Shimei and their wives, and all the rest of the clans and their wives. (emphasis added)

In Zechariah's call for repentance, it is clear that true repentance cannot be reduced to mere words but must be accompanied by genuine sorrow (cf. 2 Cor 7:7–9). Repetition can help us identify the tone or chief motifs of a passage.

Besides the reiteration of words, aspects of grammar can be repeated, as is the case in Psalm 95:1–7a:

Oh come, *let us sing* (Hebrew cohortative) to the LORD; *let us make a joyful noise* (Hebrew cohortative) to the rock of our salvation! *Let us come* (Hebrew cohortative) into his presence with thanksgiving; *let us make a joyful noise* (Hebrew cohortative) to him with songs of praise! For the LORD is a great God, and a great King above all gods. In his hand are the depths of the earth; the heights of the mountains are his also. The sea is his, for he made it, and his hands formed the dry land. Oh come, *let us worship* (Hebrew cohortative) and *bow down* (Hebrew cohortative); *let us kneel* (Hebrew cohortative) before the LORD, our Maker! For he is our God, and we are the people of his pasture, and the sheep of his hand.

The first-person plural exhortation (the Hebrew cohortative) appears seven times. While the second part of this psalm (vv. 7b–11) deals with warning and rebuke, the first section contains this sevenfold exhortation to worship God. The first four commands are more exuberant and rooted in God being the transcendent, sovereign Creator. The final three are more reverential and rest on God being our close, personal Shepherd. In a sermon, then, these kinds of nuances would constitute a subpoint to a main one. God's unconditional covenant with Abram in Genesis 12 is characterized as an expression of divine blessing, which the preacher could go on to explain further. Or in the case of Zechariah 12, true repentance involves mourning, and you could then unpack this aspect of the emotional dimension of biblical repentance.

Word Order

Another simple way the biblical writers create nuance is through word order or position. In English, the standard word order is subject-verb-object, e.g., "I finished my paper." While we might possibly say something like "My paper I finished," we would never say, "Finished I my paper" (although Yoda might). While secular Koine Greek word order is subject-verb-object, the Koine Greek of the New Testament has the word order of verb-subject-object because of the influence of the Jewish Scriptures on the New Testament authors: Hebrew (also reflected in the LXX) uses the same order.[4] Whenever the author alters this verb-subject-object order—when a word gets shifted to the front of the clause—this would emphasize the "fronted" word.

One of the most beloved passages in all of Scripture, Psalm 23 opens with "The LORD is my shepherd" (v. 1a). It can be a useful exercise to recite this verse by emphasizing a different word each time and explain the implications of each: The *Lord* is my shepherd. The Lord *is* my shepherd. The Lord is *my* shepherd. The Lord is my *shepherd*. David, however, in Psalm 23:1a, emphasizes one word and only one word by virtue of the Hebrew word order: "The LORD" (יהוה), Yahweh. Yahweh, and Yahweh alone, is David's shepherd; the rest of the psalm unpacks how he shepherds him.

Fronting also occurs in the opening line of John's Gospel: "In the beginning was the Word; and the Word was with God, and the Word was God" (John 1:1). The verse is composed of three small sentences:

---

4. See the discussion of word order in N. Turner, *A Grammar of the New Testament,* ed. J. Moulton, vol. 3, *Syntax* (Edinburgh: T&T Clark, 1993), 347–48.

Ἐν ἀρχῇ ἦν ὁ λόγος
καὶ ὁ λόγος ἦν πρὸς τὸν θεόν
καὶ θεὸς ἦν ὁ λόγος

Fronting occurs in each clause. In the first, Ἐν ἀρχῇ ("In the beginning") is fronted: The Word has existed *from the very beginning.* In the second it is ὁ λόγος ("the Word"): The one who was with God was *the Word.* In the final sentence, θεός ("God") is fronted for emphasis: And this Word was none other than *God.*

There are a few words that frequently appear in Greek that grammarians refer to as "post-positive," meaning they can never be the first word in a sentence although they are usually translated in English as the first word: δέ ("and," "but," "now"), γάρ ("for," "because"), and οὖν ("therefore"). The word or phrase that precedes a post-positive would be considered emphatic. Thus, for example, in Philippians 1:8, when Paul states, μάρτυς γάρ μου ὁ θεός ὡς ἐπιποθῶ πάντας ὑμᾶς ἐν σπλάγχνοις Χριστοῦ Ἰησοῦ ("God is my witness how I long for all of you with the mercies of Christ Jesus," ESV), by placing μάρτυς in front of the post-positive γάρ, Paul emphasizes in this sentence how he relates to God or how God stands behind him as he writes his letter: God is his *witness.* Again, after Paul updates the Philippian church on how their own church member, Epaphroditus, almost died on the mission field while serving them, Paul admonishes the church in Philippians 2:29a: προσδέχεσθε οὖν αὐτὸν ἐν κυρίῳ μετὰ πάσης χαρᾶς ("So receive him in the Lord with all joy," ESV). By fronting προσδέχεσθε, Paul emphasizes how they are to act toward Epaphroditus now that he has returned to them: they are to *receive* him, not complain about him (for falling ill while on the job) or dispute with him (cf. Phil 2:14).[5] Syntactical emphases

---

5. Philippians 2:14: "Do everything without grumbling or arguing." Paul's allusion to Deuteronomy 32:5 in 2:15 may even suggest that some of the congregation

reveal important nuances of the author that should make their presence felt in the sermon. But beyond a statement as to what effect the emphasis produces—similar to the way these emphases are handled in the examples above—there would not be enough to constitute an entire subpoint in the sermon.

Purpose/Result Clauses

Another important word that helps the exegete to understand the author's flow of thought is ἵνα ("in order that," "so that," "that"). Chiefly, ἵνα introduces a clause (called the "ἵνα clause") that can indicate either purpose or result (or sometimes both). Thus, for example, in his second prayer for that church, Paul tells the Ephesians that he bows before God the Father in prayer (Eph 3:14–15) ἵνα—"in order that" or "so that," i.e., indicating purpose—God would, from out of his glorious riches, give to them power by his Spirit in their inner being (3:16). Generally, context would determine whether a ἵνα clause indicates purpose or result. When Jesus and his disciples encounter the blind man in John 9, they enquire, "Rabbi, who sinned—this man or his parents, that (ἵνα) he was born blind?" (v. 2). Clearly, ἵνα here indicates result, not purpose: the disciples believe that blindness has resulted from personal sin.

Hebrew scholar Robert Chisholm lists the different ways that Hebrew indicates purpose or result (i.e., a kind of Hebrew equivalent for the ἵνα clause):

- ל ("to" or "for") prefixed to an infinitive construct

- למען ("in order that" or "for the sake of")

- בעבור ("so that" or "for the sake of")

---

were grumbling against their leaders the way the Israelites grumbled against Moses.

- אשר ("so that" or "with the result that")

- פֶּן ("lest")

- בלתי ("lest") (if negated)[6]

For example, after God created Adam (Gen 2:15): "The LORD God took the man and put him in the garden of Eden to work it (לעבדה) and keep it (לשמרה)"—a ל prefixed to an infinitive construct, indicating purpose. Depending on the nature of the text, the unpacking of a purpose or result clause could constitute a whole subpoint in the homily for a main one. Thus, here in the second creation account God places Adam in the garden for the expressed purpose of working and maintaining it. More broadly, then, in view of the first creation account, God has created humanity to be his image bearers in the world, ruling it by cultivating and developing creation. This could be unpacked further.

In the Old Testament, the Hebrew equivalent for ὅτι would be the causal prepositions, כי, על, יען, and אשר, each of which is typically translated as "for," "because" "since," or the like.[7] Thus, for example, God rebukes the serpent in the garden, "Because (כי) you have done this, cursed are you above all livestock and above all beasts of the field; on your belly you shall go, and dust you shall eat all the days of your life" (Gen 3:14). Or again when Samuel rebukes King Saul, he says, "Because (יען) you have rejected the word of the LORD, he has also rejected you from being king" (1 Sam 15:23).

---

6. Chisholm, *Exegesis to Exposition*, 116. Cf. Bruce Waltke and M. O'Connor, *An Introduction to Biblical Hebrew Syntax* (Winona Lake, IN: Eisenbrauns, 1990), 38.3.

7. Cf. Chisholm, *Exegesis to Exposition*, 116.

GRAMMATICAL NUANCES

Greek Verb Tense

Verb tenses can offer significant insights into a New Testament text. However, we need to exercise caution to avoid certain exegetical pitfalls. Dan Wallace, for example, speaks of the "abused aorist": when preachers make far more of the aorist tense than they rightly should.[8] Many grammarians now recognize that the aorist tense (often translated as a simple past tense) is perhaps the least aspectually significant of the Greek tenses. In other words, when the author does not want to draw particular attention to the verb, he will often use the aorist. For example, consider the familiar verse Romans 3:23: "For all have sinned and fall short of the glory of God" (πάντες γὰρ ἥμαρτον καὶ ὑστεροῦνται τῆς δόξης τοῦ θεοῦ). By using the aorist for "sinned" (ἥμαρτον), Paul deflects attention away from the activities that constitute sin, thereby keeping it in the background. This deflection receives confirmation from the fact that, on the one hand, "all" (πάντες) is fronted in the verse and is therefore being emphasized. On the other hand, the wider context beginning in Romans 3:9 underscores the comprehensiveness of human sin: all sin, each and every human being.[9] If Paul had wanted to stress the activities comprising "sin" in 3:23, he would have either fronted the verb or used a different tense rather than simply the aorist, or he could have done both. The fronting of "all" as well as the co-text indicate that Paul is stressing the

---

8. Daniel Wallace, *The Basics of New Testament Syntax: An Intermediate Greek Grammar* (Grand Rapids: Zondervan, 2001), 240.

9. Thus, the apostle writes, "Jews and Gentiles alike are all under the power of sin. As it is written: 'There is no one righteous, not even one; there is no one who understands; there is no one who seeks God. All have turned away, they have together become worthless; there is no one who does good, not even one'" (Rom 3:9b–12).

universality of sin (*all* have sinned), rather than the rebellious activities of humanity (that all have *sinned*).

The first set of Greek tenses that ought to cause us to pause are the perfect and pluperfect. Because these two verb forms appear only infrequently in the New Testament, when the biblical author deploys them, your antenna should automatically go up. There are, however, a small handful of verbs that normally operate out of the perfect, and hence as far as these particular words are concerned, the perfect tense would not be significant.[10] The perfect tense describes a past, completed event that has ongoing or abiding results stretching into the present (in relation to the author of the text).[11] Paul, for example, concludes his intercessory prayer for the Philippians with, "filled (πεπληρωμένοι) with the fruit of righteousness that comes through Jesus Christ" (Phil 1:11). The perfect tense he employs for "filled," would refer to a past, completed action with ongoing results. What would be the past, completed righteousness-imparting event that Paul refers to? The moment the Philippians first turned to Christ for salvation, the "good work" God began (Phil 1:6) when Paul first preached there ten years earlier (cf. Acts 16). The ongoing or abiding results would be their sanctification: the believers' increasing harvest of righteousness (holiness, Christlikeness) that Jesus works out in them through his Holy Spirit.

A second set of tenses that can be significant are the imperfect and the present. While not as rare as the perfect, the imperfect nevertheless appears relatively infrequently in the New

---

10. Wallace refers to these words as "perfects with a present force" (Wallace, *Syntax*, 249–50). By far the most common of these would be οἶδα ("to know"), which constitutes approximately one-quarter of all occurrences of the perfect tense in the New Testament.

11. See Wallace, *Syntax*, 246.

Testament.[12] By contrast, the present tense occurs regularly. The present and imperfect essentially depict an action from the inside as a process.[13] In motion picture terms, it would be like a movie scene where the camera focuses on what the actor/actress is doing: walking on the sand, riding a bike, running through the street, etc. It is not simply that the person has walked on the beach or ridden down a road or run down a street—this sort of summary idea of an action would be conveyed by the aorist, which would offer a snapshot or picture of these actions. Rather, with the imperfect and present we are watching a person in the process of walking on a beach, riding down a road, or running down the street. Thus, a verb in the imperfect or present tense often carries the sense of repetition or habituality. John describes how, after the authorities flogged Jesus and dressed him up as a pretend king, "They *came* (imperfect tense) up to Him and *said* (imperfect tense), 'Hail, King of the Jews'" (John 19:3 NASB). The soldiers did not walk up to Jesus once, say, "Hail, King of the Jews," and then go on to the next item of business. The twin imperfect Greek verbs imply that they kept doing this over and over. Or again, in Mark 16, the women on their way to the tomb "*asked* (imperfect tense) each other, 'Who will roll the stone away from the entrance of the tomb?'" (Mark 16:3). While walking along to the tomb they did not simply ask this question once. The imperfect implies that it was an ongoing concern for them. They likely went back and forth on the matter as they walked along, trying to think of people who could help them do it.

---

12. See the data offered by Wallace, *Syntax*, 214.

13. This would be the opposite of, say, the aorist, which depicts an action from the outside as a completed act.

In narrative texts especially, sometimes the present can be deployed not with this ongoing sense but as a way of making a story more vivid. In fact, Bible translations typically translate these present tense usages as a past. In Mark 16, when the women see the angel, "He said (present tense) to them, 'Do not *be alarmed* (present tense). You *seek* (present tense) Jesus of Nazareth'" (v. 6 ESV). The second two present tenses are easily explained: the women in the moment are alarmed and at that moment they are searching for Jesus. Bible translations, however, translate the first present tense as past referring, as "said."[14] The idea behind the use of the present here has to do with making the story more vivid—one of the marks of good storytelling. A present used in this way, called a "historical present," functions as a means of drawing the reader into the story.[15] Verb tense, then, reveals important nuances of the author that should make their presence felt in the sermon: a simple statement describing the effect that the tense produces would suffice. For example, in preaching Matthew 1:18–25, the verb used to describe Joseph's refraining from sexual relations with Mary is an imperfect tense (v. 25a). The imperfect implies not simply the end result but the duration of his abstinence: Joseph faithfully kept Mary's virginity intact over the course of her nine-month pregnancy. The imperfect, then, gives us the picture of an "ongoingness" to Joseph's commitment to Mary's (and his) sexual purity.

---

14. See, for example, the NIV, NASB, NLT, ESV.

15. We often do this in our own storytelling. When recounting a harrowing or frustrating auto experience, for example, we might refer to a past incident in the present: "And then, as I was merging into traffic, this crazy driver *cuts me off!*"

Voice

Grammatical voice can play an important role in exegesis, especially the passive voice. In some contexts, the passive voice is used as an oblique way of referring to God as the subject or the performer of an action. Grammarians refer to this usage as the "theological" or "divine passive." Returning to Paul's prayer for the Philippians, he prays that they would be "filled (πεπληρωμένοι) with the fruit of righteousness that comes through Jesus Christ" (1:11). Besides being a perfect-tense participle (as previously noted), it is also passive in voice. In other words, the expectation is not that believers would fill themselves with righteousness; rather, God is the one who has filled them—from the moment of their conversion—and continues to fill them until now (and who will continue to do so; cf. 1:6). This is further reinforced in the verse with the phrase, "that comes through Jesus Christ": the righteousness they experience originates with Jesus's work in them. Similarly, in Paul's second prayer for the Ephesians, he prays that they would be "rooted (passive voice) and established (passive voice) in love" (3:17). These two passive voice participles imply that God does this for the believer: hence, Paul's petition—to call on God to do for the church what only he can do. Like with verb tense, a simple statement or two describing the effect that the passive voice produces would be all that is needed for the sermon. In preaching Matthew 1:18–25, you could mention the passive voices of the two verbs used to describe the fulfillment of Scripture in verse 22: "fulfill" and "spoken." Here, the theological passive would be in play. God is the one who sovereignly brings about the fulfillment of Scripture, and God is the one who spoke directly through the prophet Isaiah.

Case

Finally, sometimes certain grammatical cases require nuancing for clarification. This is particularly the case (pardon the pun) for the genitive and dative forms. The simple translation for the genitive is "of"; for example, the opening words of the book of Revelation: Ἀποκάλυψις Ἰησοῦ Χριστοῦ: "The revelation *of* Jesus Christ" (ESV). Grammarians note, however, that the genitive case is very elastic and covers a great deal of ground, semantically speaking. Wallace understands the genitive to have twenty-seven distinct possible nuances.[16] Periodically, greater nuancing can yield a deeper understanding. In the first line of Revelation, "The revelation of Jesus Christ" (ESV), the genitive (Ἰησοῦ Χριστοῦ) might be interpreted as source, that is, "from": the revelation that John receives originates from the risen Lord. It could be a subjective genitive, whereby Jesus himself is the one who reveals the revelation to John; or perhaps an objective genitive: Jesus (and not the Father or the Spirit) is the object or the content of the revelation to John—in other words, it is all fundamentally about Jesus. Maybe it is merely possessive: it is Jesus Christ's revelation—it belongs to him. While this sort of nuancing does not necessarily produce earth-shattering observations, it nevertheless can affect, at least in part, the exegete's outlook on Revelation.

Like the genitive, the dative case is also very pliable.[17] Occasionally, how we understand a particular dative usage can be quite insightful. Many Christians have memorized all or part of the popular verse, "I have been crucified with Christ and I no longer live, but Christ lives in me. The life I now live

---

16. Wallace, *Syntax*, 43–64.

17. Wallace, *Syntax*, 65–80, lists nineteen different uses of the dative.

in the body, I live by faith in the Son of God, who loved me and gave himself for me" (Gal 2:20). Believers have assumed for ages that when Paul says "Christ lives in me," he is speaking spatially. In other words, Jesus lives inside of every Christian. While there are many texts that teach the indwelling presence of Christ in the believer, should this verse be added to that list? The phrase in question employs a dative: Christ lives ἐν ἐμοὶ ("in me"). Doubtless, ἐμοί is in the dative because ἐν has put it there (as it does with all of its direct objects). But is there more to the story? It is possible, even probable, that ἐν ἐμοὶ serves as the Koine equivalent for the older Classical Greek use of the "naked" dative—that is, ἐμοί by itself.[18] How, then, could the dative ἐμοί/ἐν ἐμοὶ in Galatians 2:20 be understood? Paul might not be speaking spatially here but referentially: Christ lives with reference to me. The thought, then, would be similar to what he writes in Philippians 1:21: "For to me (ἐμοί), to live is Christ and to die is gain." In other words, Paul declares something like, "As far as I'm concerned, to live is Christ." Paul's ultimate goal, his chief objective in life, is to glorify Jesus with his entire being. Once again, the effect of the grammatical case need only be limited to a single statement in the sermon. Thus, if I were to preach from Philippians 1:27–30, I would note that the relational struggles or conflicts that Paul describes as taking place "in" him (ἐν ἐμοὶ; v. 30) refers not to internal forces but external ones: he and his gospel are the flashpoint for what he's having to endure.

---

18. Greek (like other languages) becomes simpler and less subtle over time. Cf. Wallace, *Syntax*, 19–20.

SEMANTIC (LEXICAL) NUANCES

I have reserved this final type of exegetical analysis for last for two reasons. First, "word studies" tend to be the go-to for Bible interpreters because they require little or, with the right tools, no knowledge of the original languages. Thus, it is all too easy to become overly and uncritically dependent on lexicons. It is actually far more important and helpful to invest time doing the other elements of exegesis. Second, there are not a few pitfalls in lexical analysis that preachers frequently fall into that merit some discussion.

What Not to Do

In his mammoth volume on hermeneutics, Grant Osborne lists a number of different semantic fallacies that exegetes and preachers commonly commit.[19] He begins by describing the lexical fallacy, where the exegete ascribes determinative priority to word studies over the immediate context as if words have an intrinsic meaning that is unaffected by their immediate context. For example, some claim that φιλέω always denotes "brotherly love,"[20] while ἀγαπάω refers to God's self-sacrificial love. But there are numerous instances where these meanings are reversed. One clear example of this occurs in 2 Samuel 13 in the LXX—the Bible for the early Christians and Greek-speaking Jews. The narrator twice states that David's son Amnon "loved" (ἀγαπάω) his sister Tamar (vv. 1, 4). And what does his "self-sacrificial love" for her lead him to do? Rape her, and afterward hate her intensely (v. 15). Clearly, ἀγαπάω by itself does not mean

---

19. See Osborne, *Spiral*, 83–93. Cf. D. A. Carson, *Exegetical Fallacies* (Grand Rapids: Baker, 1984), 23–66.

20. As in "Philadelphia," nicknamed "the city of brotherly love."

"self-sacrificial love."[21] This kind of lexical fallacy leads to what Old Testament scholar James Barr called "illegitimate totality transfer": the exegete reads all or most of the possible meanings of a word into that single passage.[22] The Amplified Bible made this interpretive error popular in the 1990s. Osborne uses the English word "grill" to demonstrate this error. When I was being "grilled" during my PhD defense, never did I associate my being grilled by my PhD committee with questions about barbecuing hamburgers, replacing the worn-out grill of our backyard fence, or with fixing the damaged front grill of my car. It's wrong to assume that "grill" can carry all of these denotations whenever it's used. As preachers, we must resist the temptation to approach the semantic field of a word like some smorgasbord of meanings, where we can just choose the meaning of the term that fits best with our personal agenda or pick the one that preaches. Lexicons list the meaning of words in descending order of frequency: the first one corresponds to the most common and most expected meaning; the last one refers to the least. We need solid, exegetical reasons for passing over a higher-ranked meaning in favor of a more obscure one. Just because a meaning is *possible* does not make it useable in every context. The further down the list a definition appears in the lexicon, the less likely that particular dictionary entry ought to be called on.

---

21. Some exegetes make the same error when they extrapolate from the text to biblical theology. James Barr writes that "the connection between [biblical language and theology] must be made in the first place at the level of the larger linguistic complexes such as the sentences. It is the sentence (and of course the still larger literary complex such as the complete speech or poem) which is the linguistic bearer of the usual theological statement, and not the word (the lexical unit) or the morphological and syntactical connection" (Barr, *The Semantics of Biblical Language* [Oxford: Oxford University Press, 1961], 263).

22. Barr, *Semantics*, 218.

Another potential pitfall for the preacher is the root fallacy: the assumption that the root word of a given term and its cognates carry the same basic meaning. Preaching on John's Upper Room Discourse of John 13–17, many a preacher has waxed eloquently on John's description of the Holy Spirit, the παράκλητος. The constituent or root words of this term, we are told, are παρά ("beside") and καλέω ("call"). Hence, the Holy Spirit ought to be thought of as the "one called alongside of." While the word may have held that meaning in earlier, Classical Greek, it had all but lost that force by the time of the New Testament. Bible translators rightly render it as either "Advocate" (befitting a legal context) or as "Counselor" (in a non-legal context).

There may be instances when examining the constituent root words sheds light on the term in question. For example, the Greek word translated "resurrection," ἀνάστασις, is composed of the prefix ἀνα, meaning "up," and the noun στάσις, "be standing," jointly yielding the idea of "standing up." Jesus entered the tomb lying down but emerged from it upright, standing on his feet. But literary context must always be the final determinant (like with παράκλητος in John 13–17).

In the etymological fallacy, the exegete assumes that a word maintains its original or source meaning. In other words, a word keeps the meaning that it had in its original, ancient context hundreds or even thousands of years later. We need not look any further than the English language, however, to see that this is clearly not the case. In the KJV, Genesis 2:24 reads, "Therefore shall a man leave his father and his mother, and shall *cleave* unto his wife: and they shall be one flesh" (emphasis added). In 1611 "cleave" meant something along the lines of "cling to" or "unite with." Centuries later, the word "cleave" now means the exact opposite: meat *cleavers* separate meat from bones and joints; in chemistry, ionic lattices *cleave*: they split apart.

Similar to the etymological fallacy, preachers often commit the one-meaning fallacy when they assume that a Greek or Hebrew word has the same meaning all the time and, therefore, there is a universal meaning to every word. Greek scholar Johannes Louw all but shatters this assumption with his insightful example of σάρξ.[23] While σάρξ is typically translated "flesh" (its common gloss in lexicons), in different contexts it has completely different meanings. In the prologue of John's Gospel, for example, the Word became σάρξ, which here means a human being (John 1:14). In Matthew's Olivet Discourse, apart from the foreshortening of persecution, no σάρξ would survive, meaning no person (Matt 24:22). In Paul's discussion of national Israel, he makes a distinction between children of the promise and children of σάρξ, that is, of natural birth (Rom 9:8). Paul can also use σάρξ to refer to the fallen, Adamic nature (Rom 8:13). The author of Hebrews refers to Jesus's incarnation as the days of his σάρξ: his earthly life (Heb 5:7). Jude speaks of Sodom and Gomorrah as giving themselves up to σάρξ, meaning sexual immorality (Jude 7). Clearly, word meanings do not exist as singular points on a number line but as line segments with a range of meaning; and which meaning a word bears in any one instance depends squarely on the context in which it appears. The perspective embedded in these last two fallacies underlies two significant lexical works: the *Theological Dictionary of the Old Testament* (*TDOT*) and the *Theological Dictionary of the New Testament* (*TDNT*). While these multivolume works can be very helpful, they have the potential to obscure the meaning of biblical words for the unsuspecting preacher because of their diachronic rather than synchronic

---

23. See Johannes Louw, *Semantics of New Testament Greek* (Philadelphia: Fortress, 1982), 39–40.

approach: what the word meant over time versus what it meant at the time of the biblical writer.

Somewhat akin to these semantic fallacies is the common error of downloading post-Reformational theology back into a biblical word as if the human author had all of that robust theology in mind when he wrote his text. When Matthew, for example, records, "For I tell you that unless your righteousness surpasses that of the Pharisees and the teachers of the law, you will certainly not enter the kingdom of heaven" (Matt 5:20), preachers often equate Jesus's use of "righteousness" here with Paul's use of the word in Romans[24]—a book that fueled the Protestant Reformation with its mantra, "Justification by faith alone." But Jesus was not thinking along such lines in the Sermon on the Mount. Pre-Easter, "righteousness" always referred to what a person ought to do: the righteous person does what he or she ought to do; the wicked do not. In fact, the very next set of verses after 5:20 (5:21–48) begin to unpack what Jesus was after, the kind of righteousness that exceeds that of the religious leaders: a righteousness in full accord with the Mosaic law that is concerned with the heart (the spirit of the law) and not simply the outward actions (the letter of the law).

Having looked at what not to do, what mistakes not to commit, how can we safely proceed when doing lexical studies?

What to Do

To begin with, two of the better lexicons to use would be Brown-Driver-Briggs (BDB) for the Old Testament and Bauer-Danker-Arndt-Gingrich (BDAG, formerly BAGD) for the

---

24. E.g., Rom 3:21–22: "But now apart from the law the righteousness of God has been made known, to which the Law and the Prophets testify. This righteousness is given through faith in Jesus Christ to all who believe."

New Testament.[25] Additionally, Grant Osborne offers some sage advice.[26] He notes, first, that we must determine the key words in the passage. All words are not created equal. While all biblical words are divinely revealed and inspired, they do not all carry the same exegetical weight: some are more important than others. New Testament scholar Gordon Fee presents four steps for identifying the key words in a passage.[27] The words that commend themselves for lexical study are those terms that:

- are "theologically loaded," e.g., words like "grace" or "salvation"

- appear crucial for understanding a passage

- are repeated in and around the passage

- become important during the process of exegesis

Consider Paul's prayer in Philippians 1:9–11:

> And this is my prayer: that your love may abound more and more in knowledge and depth of insight, so that you may be able to discern what is best and may be pure and blameless for the day of Christ, filled with the fruit of righteousness that comes through Jesus Christ—to the glory and praise of God.

Doubtless, the most theologically loaded word (especially for Paul) would be "righteousness" (δικαιοσύνη); there are the terms "love" (ἀγάπη), "Christ" (Χριστός), and "glory" (δόξα). In terms of non-loaded words that are important for

---

25. See "Resources" below for the full bibliographic information.

26. See Osborne, *Spiral*, 108–12.

27. Gordon Fee, *New Testament Exegesis: A Handbook for Students and Pastors* (Grand Rapids: Zondervan, 1983), 84–85.

understanding the text: perhaps "abound" (περισσεύω) and "knowledge" (ἐπίγνωσις). Words that Paul repeats in and around this passage, or that appear frequently elsewhere, and/or that become important in the process of exegesis include: "prayer" (προσεύχομαι),[28] "glory"[29] (although this word has already been identified as important for theological reasons), "the day of Christ,"[30] and "fill" (πληρόω). Although BDAG will list the occurrences of Greek words, a Greek concordance (software or hardcopy) can also prove beneficial here to see how the words are used elsewhere.

From the Old Testament, consider Job 42:1–6:

> Then Job answered the LORD and said: "I know that you can do all things, and that no purpose of yours can be thwarted. 'Who is this that hides counsel without knowledge?' Therefore I have uttered what I did not understand, things too wonderful for me, which I did not know. 'Hear, and I will speak; I will question you, and you make it known to me.' I had heard of you by the hearing of the ear, but now my eye sees you; therefore I despise myself, and repent in dust and ashes."

In this text the only "theologically loaded" term would be "LORD" (יהוה). Non-loaded words that are important for understanding this passage might be "purpose" (מזמה), "thwarted" (בצר), "counsel" (עצה), "knowledge" (דעת), "wonderful" (פלא), "despise" (מאס), and "repent" (נחם). Another word that ought to be examined because of its frequency in the passage is ידע

---

28. While προσεύχομαι is not used elsewhere, synonyms appear in vv. 3–4.

29. Cf. Phil 2:11; 3:19, 21; 4:19, 20.

30. Cf. Phil 1:5, 6; 2:16

("know"), which occurs twice in verse 2 and once in 3, as well as its cognate (דעת), also in verse 3.

Second, as Fee notes, you must determine the semantic range of the key words. Crucial to this determination is the synchronic dimension of the word—what it meant at the time the biblical author used it—rather than how it was used throughout its history (diachronic, as interesting as that might be). In Classical Greek, for example, ἄλλος ("other") applied strictly to the same kind of a thing (e.g., the red apple and the "other" one that is green), while ἕτερος ("other") applied to a different kind of a thing (e.g., the apple versus the "other" fruit, the banana). In Koine Greek, however, no such clear-cut distinction exists, and the words are often deployed interchangeably. In Matthew's Gospel, when Jesus asks his disciples what people are saying about who he is, they reply, "Some say John the Baptist; others (ἄλλος) say Elijah; and still others (ἕτερος), Jeremiah or one of the prophets" (Matt 16:14). Clearly, it would be wrong to assume that Jesus intends some big distinction between these two groups. Each believes Jesus is one of the prophets of yore come back to life. The two words are merely deployed interchangeably for the sake of stylistic variation.

You also need to carefully consider the context in which the key words appear. Osborne writes, "Note how the word fits into the total statement of the passage and try to elucidate the influence of the surrounding terms on it."[31] By doing this, you will avoid the trap of illegitimate totality transfer.[32] In Philippians 1:9–11, looking up ἐπίγνωσις will yield a semantic range of meaning. Not all meanings would be appropriate to

---

31. Osborne, *Spiral*, 110.

32. This step does not apply to theologically loaded words but to the other ones; see the discussion of sense and reference below.

read into that word here. That Paul pairs ἐπίγνωσις with αἴθησις ("insight") suggests that the meaning for ἐπίγνωσις is informed by its pairing with αἴθησις. That the two words agree in gender, number, and case, and are joined together by a καί, suggests that Paul uses the two words to convey a single idea, not two different ones.[33] In Job 42:1–6, the meanings of the Hebrew words for "purpose," "counsel," and "knowledge" in verses 2 and 3 would inform each other. The parallel structure in verse 3 means that the Hebrew term for "know" ought to be constrained by the word for "understand."[34] Similarly, the *waw* (ו) directly connects "despise" to "repent," so these two words should be understood relative to each other.

Third, and related to discerning theologically loaded terms, you must determine whether a word is used primarily in terms of its sense or its reference. On the one hand, by "reference," scholars mean a word is deployed in a technical or semi-technical way—something of a trade name. Osborne notes, "Many New Testament words had a semitechnical force that derived its meaning from the life of the early church as much as from Hellenistic usage. In those cases we must at all times be aware of the Christian meaning inherent [in some terms]."[35] The words ἀγάπη and ἀγαπάω appear frequently throughout the LXX, and while translated "love," the words have a broad enough semantic field to even denote "lust" (as observed in 2 Sam 13). The earliest followers of Christ, however, took over this word

---

33. This would be a Granville Sharp construction. See Wallace, *Syntax*, 120–28.

34. The verse reflects the classic, poetic A-B- A'- B'- parallelism:

   "Therefore, I have uttered
       what I did not understand (בין),
   things too wonderful for me,
       which I did not know (ידע)."

35. Osborne, *Spiral*, 111.

group and charged ἀγάπη/ἀγαπάω with the essential meaning of self-sacrificial love, thus becoming a kind of "trade name" for certain Christian activities. Referential words automatically assume a place of importance in the text in which they appear and therefore must be examined. Osborne recommends they are best studied conceptually rather than structurally from the passage in which they appear. Thus, in Paul's prayer in Philippians 1:9–11, when he prays that the believers' "love" (ἀγάπη) would grow, while the passage serves to unpack what that might look like, since ἀγάπη has become a technical term by the time Paul writes, it would be correct to define "love" here as the self-sacrificial love Christ demonstrated by his incarnation (cf. Phil 2:6–8). That understanding of the term does not come directly out of Paul's text here, but it would be well understood to carry this meaning for the earliest Christians. Still, Osborne urges us to exercise care in this conceptual analysis and not to read more into the word than the context allows.

On the other hand, if an author deploys a word according to its sense, then it is studied structurally from its context. Its meaning depends squarely on the meaning it receives from the literary context in which it appears. Such would be the case for most words you encounter.

Because of their obvious accessibility, you need to resist the temptation to allow your homily to become overrun with word studies. It would be better to convey the nuances offered by such studies with a few summary statements rather than expanding them into sermon subpoints.

Here is one example of how this works out in practice. In Job 42:1–6, after God speaks to Job from out of the storm, reminding him of his transcendent character, "Job replied to the LORD: 'I know that you can do all things'" (vv.1–2a NIV). Job confesses that he now knows of God's limitless power; but the Hebrew word translated "know" tells us more. In your sermon, you could point out that the term does not merely refer to mental assent—"to know about." Rather, it denotes knowing something experientially—to know it from the heart (intimately, emotionally). The same Hebrew word is used, for example, to denote sexual union between Adam and Eve: "Adam *made love to*"—literally, "knew"—"his wife Eve, and she became pregnant" (Gen 4:1a NIV; cf. 4:17a, 25a). Job, then, far from just intellectually or philosophically acknowledging God's omnipotence, has come to know and experience this truth from the heart.

CONCLUSION

These, then, are the minutiae that every exegete must deal with. New Testament scholar Michael Gorman offers a wonderful illustration of what the minutiae of exegetical analysis accomplish:

> In some ways, exegesis is like doing a puzzle. To put together a puzzle, you must find and arrange the small pieces (details) in order to create a picture (the whole). The process involves identifying the parts and discovering how they fit together. Without the little pieces, there would be no puzzle picture. But the little pieces alone are only a very small part of the picture; their ultimate value lies in their contribution to the larger picture.[36]

The exegetical details will fill out the sermon outline. In other words, the details of the analysis represent subpoints or perhaps sub-subpoints that give the sermon a greater depth for teaching. While churches address the issue of spiritual growth

---

36. Michael Gorman, *Elements of Biblical Exegesis: A Basic Guide for Students and Ministers,* 3rd ed. (Grand Rapids: Baker Academic, 2020), 110–11.

in a myriad of ways, the pulpit should offer another means of bringing about spiritual growth in the congregation. Good preaching must speak to the heart, rousing our emotions in accordance with the truth or attribute of God being exposited. But it must also speak to the mind—to the intellect. The exegetical minutiae engage the worshiper's mind, something that should characterize the life of the believer, as the "Great Commandment" affirms: "The Lord our God, the Lord is one. Love the Lord your God with all your heart and with all your soul and with *all your mind* and with all your strength' " (Mark 12:29, emphasis added).

Minutiae matter. But there are two important caveats. First, the point of this attention to the finer points of the original language is not to "wow" the audience. Nor is it for the preacher to show off what a fine seminary or Bible college education can do for a Christian. The purpose of thoughtfully engaging with the minutiae is to teach the flock, to deepen their faith, to help them love God with their mind. Second, this part of the sermon process can be fraught with grammatical jargon. This jargon needs to be left on the cutting room floor of the study. Explaining to the congregation, for example, the term "post-positive" is unnecessary and ought to be avoided. The end product of word emphasis—based on what precedes the post-positive—would be all that matters for the homily.

Having drilled down into the finer details of the text, we can now once again peer outside the sermon passage, this time to the other parts of Scripture.

RESOURCES

Accordance Bible Software. Altamonta Springs: OakTree Software. https://accordancebible.com/site-licenses-and-academic-program/.

Bauer, W. *A Greek-English Lexicon of the New Testament and Other Early Christian Literature*. 3rd ed. Edited by F. Danker. Chicago: University of Chicago, 2000.

Blass, F., A. Debrunner, and R. Funk. *A Greek Grammar of the New Testament and other Early Christian Literature*. Chicago: University of Chicago Press, 1961.

Brown, F., S. Driver, and C. Briggs. *The New Brown, Driver, Briggs, Gesenius Hebrew and English Lexicon*. Peabody: Hendrickson, 1979.

Chisholm, R. *From Exegesis to Exposition: A Practical Guide to Using Biblical Hebrew*. Grand Rapids: Baker, 1998.

GRAMCORD. Battle Ground: The GRAMCORD Institute. http://www.gramcord.org/.

Liddell, H., and R. Scott. *A Greek-English Lexicon with a Revised Supplement*. Oxford: Clarendon Press, 1996.

Logos Bible Software. Bellingham, WA: Logos Research Systems. https://www.logos.com/academic.

Louw, J., and E. Nida, eds. *Greek-English Lexicon of the New Testament Based on Semantic Domains*. 2 vols. 2nd ed. New York: United Bible Societies, 1989.

Moulton, H. *A Concordance to the Greek New Testament*. 5th ed. Edinburgh: T&T Clark, 1978.

Mounce, W. *The Analytical Lexicon to the Greek New Testament*. Zondervan Greek Reference Series. Grand Rapids: Zondervan, 1993.

Roger, C., and C. Rogers. *The New Linguistic and Exegetical Key to the Greek New Testament*. Grand Rapids: Zondervan, 1998.

Silva, M. *God, Language and Scripture*. Foundations of Contemporary Interpretation. Edited by M. Silva. Grand Rapids: Zondervan, 1990.

Wallace, D. *The Basics of New Testament Syntax: An Intermediate Grammar; The Abridgement of Greek Grammar Beyond the Basics*. Grand Rapids: Zondervan, 2000.

CHAPTER 7

MAKING THEOLOGICAL CONNECTIONS

HOW THE TEXT RELATES TO THE REST OF SCRIPTURE

THE APOSTLE PAUL had some pointed words for Timothy as it related to his protégé discharging his duties as a preacher/ teacher of God's flock:

> Command and teach these things. ... Until I come, devote yourself to the public reading of Scripture, to preaching and to teaching. (1 Tim 4:11–13)

> Watch your life and doctrine closely. Persevere in them, because if you do, you will save both yourself and your hearers. (1 Tim 4:16)

> Do your best to present yourself to God as one approved, a worker who does not need to be ashamed and who correctly handles the word of truth. (2 Tim 2:15)

> Preach the word; be prepared in season and out of season; correct, rebuke and encourage—with great patience and careful instruction. (2 Tim 4:2)

The assumption behind Paul's strong exhortations for Timothy to preach God's word is encapsulated in 2 Timothy 3:16–17: "All Scripture is God-breathed and is useful for teaching, rebuking, correcting and training in righteousness, so that the servant of God may be thoroughly equipped for every good work." Because Scripture is "God-breathed," it has divine power to transform the lives of Jesus's followers. The same is true today. Consequently, more and more Christian scholars are recognizing the importance of theological exegesis: interpreting the Bible as a repository of God's unified self-revelation, allowing it to speak to the church for the purpose of its transformation, through deeply reflecting on and faithfully performing Scripture.

Michael Gorman examines eight principles for the theological interpretation of Scripture.[1] The key principle for the present chapter is learning how to read and understand the sermon text within its canonical context. Because Scripture is not simply a human document but, fundamentally, a divine one, there is an intrinsic unity to the diverse texts that comprise it. Scripture is the story of God's acts in bringing about salvation for his people, culminating for all times in the Christ event. There is tremendous value, then, in exploring the theological links between a sermon passage and the rest of Scripture. However, the extent to which these canonical connections find an appropriate place to rest in the sermon depends in large measure on the time allotted for the message.

---

1. Michael Gorman, *Elements of Biblical Exegesis: A Basic Guide for Students and Ministers,* 3rd ed. (Grand Rapids: Baker Academic, 2020), 163–71.

Some preachers have the luxury of preaching for forty-five to sixty minutes. In those instances, you are able to bring quite a few of these ties into the message, and by doing so, the congregation's biblical and theological vision expands and the intellectual dimension to their faith can grow. Worshiping God must never mean checking our brains at the door. Rather, worship involves engaging our minds with rigorous thought and reflection. Theological exegesis encourages this reflective process.

But many of us who preach have not been afforded an hour for the sermon. The typical allotment ranges closer to twenty-five to thirty-five minutes. Does that mean, then, that this step should be avoided because there is no room at the pulpit inn for these theological insights? On the contrary, we should still engage in this phase of moving from exegesis to exposition. It is just that, for many of us, most of the work done at this stage gets left behind on the cutting room floor of the study, never finding its way into the sermon. So then, why do it?

Ultimately, it is for your sake. Exegesis involves a lot of narrowly focused work, a lot of minutiae gazing. This is vital for an accurate interpretation of the biblical text, but there is a temptation to get lost in the weeds of a passage and fail to see the theological forest through the exegetical trees. The entirety of Scripture revolves around the metanarrative of God accomplishing salvation for his people: creation, fall, redemption. The individual books of the Bible unfold these themes in various ways, sometimes laying stress on one particular dimension of God's story, and within that stress the biblical author often puts further emphasis on related subthemes. As you connect the sermon text with other, related passages, this helps you not to lose sight of Scripture's grand metanarrative.

This type of reflection also serves to strengthen your overall grasp of Scripture, which all exegetes should continually be striving to improve. Surely, this is at least part of what the apostle Paul had in mind when he counseled Pastor Timothy, "But as for you, continue in what you have learned and have become convinced of, because you know those from whom you learned it, and how from infancy you have known the Holy Scriptures, which are able to make you wise for salvation through faith in Christ Jesus" (2 Tim 3:14–15). Therefore, even though most of the work at this stage might get left behind in the study and not make it into the pulpit, it nevertheless remains a vital part of your personal biblical and theological development. And as the preacher grows, so grows the flock.

After completing the previous five steps of exegetical analysis (described in chapters 2–6 above), you are now in the position to ask how the sermon text relates to other Scriptures, how it relates to other passages—the "canonical context."[2] In other words, you put the sermon passage in conversation with other Bible passages. This facet of study is not the same as cross-referencing. Cross-referencing compares one text with other passages—most often those suggested in the margins of English study Bibles. This type of Bible reading can be very helpful for the devotional reading of Scripture, as church planter Will Anderson writes, "Cross references slow us down, sparking reflection and critical thinking, as we explore connections between passages."[3] Many folks have benefitted greatly from the popular Thompson Chain Reference Study Bible. In the margins beside the Scripture text are plenty of related Bible references for the reader to look up and compare

---

2. So Walter Kaiser, *Toward an Exegetical Theology: Biblical Exegesis for Preaching and Teaching* (Grand Rapids: Baker, 1981), 79.

3. Will Anderson, "Cross References: Unsung Heroes of Bible Reading" The Gospel Coalition, April 16, 2021, https://www.thegospelcoalition.org/article/cross-references-unsung-heroes-bible-reading/.

with the passage at hand. For example, in the margins of Paul's prayer in Philippians 1:9–11 appear texts like Hebrews 2:11; Colossians 1:11; 1 Thessalonians 1:5; Colossians 1:27; Ephesians 5:18; 1 Peter 5:11; 2 Peter 3:18; and Jude 25. The problem as it relates to exegesis, though, is twofold. One, Paul couldn't really have had all these texts in mind when he offered his prayer to the Philippians (not least because some were written after Philippians). And even if he did have some in mind, how would Paul's original audience have gained access to these other texts that apparently inform his prayer for them? Two, the chain-reference method seems to shift interpretive control over to the reader rather than residing with the author of the biblical text.[4]

A more controlled way of engaging in intertextual conversations is to allow the text itself to set the parameters. In this approach, the biblical dialogue spirals outward. It begins with a conversation with similar texts within the same book; it then moves out to other passages or books by that same author; then onward to the rest of the New Testament (if it is a New Testament text), and, finally, to the entire canon. When reaching beyond the sermon passage to find biblical conversation partners, one way of finding other Scriptures is by looking in the apparatus of the Greek New Testament. The apparatus will list a few other relevant texts. For example, for Philippians 2:14 ("Do everything without grumbling or arguing"), the United Bible Society Greek New Testament lists 1 Corinthians 10:10 ("And do not grumble, as some of them did—and were killed by the destroying angel") and 1 Peter 4:9 ("Offer hospitality to one another without grumbling") because all three texts use the same Greek word for "grumble." The UBS will

---

4. Anderson's words paint a picture of this dynamic when he talks about the reader following "a meandering trail across the sprawling pages of Scripture."

list Old Testament texts that a New Testament passage either cites or alludes to; for example, for Philippians 2:15, it lists Deuteronomy 32:5 as the text Paul alludes to in that verse. Academic commentaries can also be quite useful for finding conversation partners. In addition to the ones listed by the Greek New Testament, Moisés Silva provides other related biblical texts for Philippians 2:14–15 in his commentary.[5]

When integrating words from the passage preached into the wider canonical context, Walter Kaiser recommends that the exegete examine the following: words that play a key role in the passage; a word that has occurred frequently in previous contexts; or important words in the history of salvation as revealed up to the point of the passage.[6] The biblical discussion partners offer different types of intertextual conversation with the sermon passage. They might reinforce or reiterate what the sermon text says. In addition to supporting the text, it might amplify or augment it, taking a point a little further theologically. A conversation partner might clarify or refine the sermon passage. Or especially when moving from Old Testament to New (or vice versa), New Testament texts will often offer clear contrast to an Old Testament passage.

Putting the sermon passage into discussion with other texts, then, serves to fill out the biblical and theological picture of the passage more than would otherwise be possible. By doing this, you expand the biblical and theological horizons of the congregation, enabling them to see and hear more clearly the harmonious unity in the voice of Scripture, and helping the flock increase in their theological understanding of the Bible

---

5. Moisés Silva, *Philippians*, Baker Exegetical Commentary on the New Testament, 2nd ed. (Grand Rapids: Baker Academic, 2005), 120–23.

6. Kaiser, *Exegetical Theology*, 143.

by modeling for them how to make appropriate connections between biblical texts. What does this look like in practice?

PHILIPPIANS 2:6–11

Philippians 2:6–11 presents a detailed christological portrait of Jesus, which can be put into conversations with smaller texts within Philippians. To begin with, verse 10 of the Christ Hymn implicitly cites Isaiah 45:23, which speaks of Yahweh as the only true God who reigns supreme over all the nations. The christological title Paul uses most frequently for Jesus is "Christ," appearing seven times in the introduction of the letter alone. How does the theology of 2:6–11 intersect with the theology embedded in the title "Christ" in Philippians? Paul speaks of the provision of "the Spirit of Jesus Christ" (1:19). How does the provision Jesus offers relate to his story encapsulated in 2:6–11? Paul refers to Jesus as "Savior" (3:20). How does that christological title dovetail with 2:6–11?

Spiraling outward beyond Philippians, because Pauline scholars regard 2:6–11 as an early Christian hymn, how does this hymn compare with other hymns like the ones in Colossians 1:15–20 or 1 Timothy 3:16? Spiraling out further, how does the content of 2:6–11 compare with other New Testament passages that speak (like Phil 2:6–11 does) of: Jesus previously existing as God (e.g., John 1:1–5; Heb 1:1–4); Jesus becoming a slave/servant (e.g., Matt 20:28); Jesus becoming a human being (e.g., the Gospels); Jesus humbling himself (e.g., Matt 11:29); Jesus dying on the cross (e.g., the passion narratives of the Gospels; Revelation 5); or of Jesus being exalted to the right hand of God (e.g., Matt 25:31–46; Acts 7:55; 1 Cor 15:23–28; Rev 5). Conversation partners like these can serve to reinforce, augment, clarify, or even contrast with and thereby highlight the christological teaching of Philippians 2:6–11.

Other than the implicit allusion to Isaiah 45:23, the Old Testament might not seem to bear immediately fruitful conversations because it is much more veiled about Christ and the incarnation than the New Testament. Spiraling out into the Old Testament does, nevertheless, yield further theological conversation partners for Philippians 2:6–11. How does Jesus previously existing in the form of God and then becoming a human being fit with the Old Testament theophanies, where a mysterious figure called "the angel of the LORD" receives worship like Yahweh (e.g., Josh 5:13–15; Judg 13:16–23)? The hymn is clear that in becoming human Jesus became a servant, so how does that intersect with the messianic Servant of Yahweh in the servant songs of Isaiah 40–55? How does the exaltation of Jesus compare or fit with the exaltation of Daniel's son of man in Daniel 7:13–14? If you were to preach the Christ hymn of Philippians 2, bringing it into theological dialogue with passages like these would force you to think more deeply and more widely, theologically speaking, which in and of itself is always beneficial. And insofar as you can bring some of these insights into the sermon, the congregation's view and understanding of the text is also expanded, causing them to reflect more widely than otherwise, thereby allowing them to see more of the sweeping metanarrative of Scripture and enabling them to appreciate the unity of the Bible behind all of its variegated literary, theological, and chronological diversity.

When it comes to preaching the Christ Hymn, many things could be said about its canonical-theological context, but I will limit myself to three comments. This hymn focuses on Jesus's humiliation in becoming a human being (vv. 6–8) and explains why Paul would use this hymn in his letter: to present Jesus as the exemplar for the humility the apostle counsels the church to walk in (see chapter 3 above). With its emphasis on the lowliness of Christ, this hymn contrasts with and complements the one in Colossians 1:15–20, which extols Christ's supremacy over all things because he is God. Finally, when speaking of Jesus's future exaltation (Phil 2:9–11), Paul's appropriation of Isaiah 45:23b ("Before me every knee will bow; by me every tongue will swear," NIV) in verses 10–11 serves to emphasize Jesus's deity. Isaiah proclaimed the universal lordship of Yahweh over the nations and their idols (Isa 44–46). By applying this text to Jesus, the apostle identifies Jesus with Yahweh (Isa 44:8: "Is there a God besides me? There is no Rock; I know not any").

MATTHEW 2:1-12

A number of aspects of this account have ready conversation partners within the wider Gospel story. The magi arrive in Jerusalem, a city whose multitudes stream to John the Baptist (Matt 3:5) and then to Jesus (4:25). Jesus calls Jerusalem the "city of the Great King" (5:35), Matthew calls it "the holy city" (27:53), and it is the place where Jesus predicts he will suffer and die (16:21; 20:17–18); consequently, he pronounces judgment upon it (21:12–20). Yet he also laments over the city because of its perpetual rejection of God's servants (23:37–39). These texts nicely augment the mention of Jerusalem in the Magi narrative. Matthew's depiction of Jerusalem could be compared with its representation by other New Testament writers like Mark, Luke, and John. In the case of Luke, for example, God's salvific activity begins in Jerusalem (1:5–23; 2:21–38, 41–49) and then cycles back there at the end of the story (24:52–53). In Acts, the mission of the church begins in Jerusalem but ultimately moves away to the nations (Acts 1:8; cf. Luke 24:47). Paul considers Jerusalem emblematic of the children of the new covenant (Gal 4:21–31). The image of Jerusalem factors significantly in the book of Revelation as a picture of the redeemed (Rev 21:10–27).

Of course, most of the biblical data for Jerusalem comes from the Old Testament, with the prophets, for example, speaking of Jerusalem as the beneficiary of future glory (e.g., Isa 54; 60) but also describing it as the repository for divine judgment (e.g., Jer 25; Ezek 22).

There is also the mixed citation in Matthew 2:6: the first part, "But you, Bethlehem, in the land of Judah, are by no means least among the rulers of Judah; for out of you will come a ruler," comes from Micah 5:2 (5:1 in the Masoretic Text), while the rest, "who will shepherd my people Israel," is from 2 Samuel 5:2. The former text prophesies of God raising up, in the wake of the ignominy of the Babylonian exile, a Davidic ruler who will shepherd God's flock in the power of the Lord despite resistance from foreign nations. In 2 Samuel 5:2, against the backdrop of Israel having previously been politically and socially divided, Yahweh appoints and confirms David as king over all Israel (and not just over Judah). God has appointed Jesus to shepherd his people, Israel. Does Matthew refer to national Israel like the Scripture texts he cites, or to "spiritual Israel," that is, the church of Jewish and Gentile believers? National Israel seems to be the case in light of what comes before in the Gospel: Israel's history depicted by way of the genealogy (1:1–17; cf. v. 21). There also seems to be development from an Israel-centric focus, highlighted by Jesus's restrictive mission to Israel (4:23–9:35) as well as by his command to his disciples to follow suit (10:5–6), to the conclusion of the Gospel where Jesus commissions his disciples to make disciples of "all the nations" (28:19). Spiraling out of Matthew to the rest of the New Testament, God's people in Luke expands to the gentiles (e.g., Luke 24:47; Acts 1:8; 15:1–35). Paul speaks of the relationship between Jewish Christians and gentile Christians (e.g., Eph 2:11–22) and between the church of Jewish and gentile

Christians and national Israel (Rom 9–11). Revelation pictorially describes God's people in very Jewish terms (Rev 7:4–8), but also as being very ethnically diverse (7:9–17).

Spiraling out into the Old Testament, the picture roughly resembles that of the New Testament. That a national-Israel emphasis runs throughout the Old Testament is without dispute, beginning with God's selection of Abram, and later affirming his elective love of national Israel from among the nations of the world (Deut 7:6–7). Nevertheless, that divine favor would eventually come to gentiles can be observed even in Israel's foundational call in Abram (Gen 12:1–3), something Paul explicitly picks up and applies to the gentile church (Gal 3:8–9, 16). The inclusion of the gentiles is also hinted at throughout the history of Israel (e.g., Josh 2; Ruth 3:13–22). Consequently, God commissions national Israel to reach the nations with the message of salvation (e.g., Ps 67; Isa 42:6; cf. Jonah). Besides the quotations from Micah 5 and 2 Samuel 5, Matthew also alludes to other Old Testament texts that can be put in theological conversation with Matthew's story. Broadly speaking, the notion of gentile royalty bearing gifts to a Jewish king echoes the account of 1 Kings 10, where the queen of Sheba offers large quantities of spices to Solomon, son of David. The gifts of "gold and incense" by the magi represent a linguistic allusion to Isaiah 60:6, which foretells of a time when tribute from the nations will be offered to Zion. The history of Israel, then, comes to be enacted in the life of Jesus.

The story of the magi contains several important christological titles ("King of the Jews," "Christ," and "Shepherd"), and these can be put into theological conversation with other texts from within Matthew, beginning with the opening line of 1:1: "This is the genealogy of Jesus the Messiah the son of David, the son of Abraham," where the messianic motifs of Shepherd and King are subsumed under the more prominent Matthean title, "son of David." Besides intersecting in the magi account, "Christ," "David" (and by extension, "Shepherd"), and "Lord" merge in Jesus's enigmatic question to the religious leaders in 22:41–46: "If then David calls [the Messiah] 'Lord,' how can he be his son?" (v. 45). The shepherd-king motif appears in the scene of final judgment in 25:31–34. Although Herod is called "king" twice (2:1, 3) before Jesus enters the story, he is never called so again despite appearing by name ten more times in the Gospel, while Jesus at his crucifixion is identified again as "the king of the Jews" (27:37, cf. v. 42), thereby echoing the title applied to him in the infancy narrative (2:2).

Spiraling outward, how does Matthew's presentation of Jesus as King, as Christ, and as Shepherd compare with that of the other New Testament writers? Matthew's Shepherd-King motif, for example, stands as unique among his Christian contemporaries. While Mark, Luke, and John deploy the shepherd metaphor, they explicitly connect it to the activity of teaching (e.g., Mark 6:34; Eph 4:11), something Matthew never does. Additionally, they minimize or eliminate altogether the pastoral imagery from the metaphor and expunge it of any geopolitical associations. Matthew does not.[7] In fact, Matthew's appropriation of the metaphor aligns more closely with how it is deployed in the Old Testament. For the Old Testament writers, the metaphor frequently depicts either earthly rulers (e.g., Num 27:17; Ps 78:70–72; Jer 23:1–4) or Yahweh (e.g., Jer 31:8–11; Ezek 34:11–16), and they typically appropriate the metaphor with

---

7. For detailed discussion of Matthew's shepherd motif, see W. Baxter, *Israel's Only Shepherd: Matthew's Shepherd Motif and His Social Setting*, Library of New Testament Studies 457 (London: T&T Clark, 2012), 97–122.

pastoral imagery (e.g., Ps 23:1; Isa 40:11) and with geopolitical associations (e.g., Jer 23:1–4; Ezek 34).

Perhaps most obviously, the entire story of the visitation of the magi can be read against Luke's birth and infancy traditions, since only here and in Luke and nowhere else in the New Testament do such accounts appear. While the content of Matthew and Luke often overlap, when it comes to the birth and infancy stories of Jesus, there is no common ground between them. A close reading of Matthew 2 (especially 2:16) indicates that chronologically it takes place between Luke 2:40 and 2:41.

Thus, putting Matthew 2:1–12 in conversation with other New Testament voices serves to augment and complement Matthew's perspective, while when set against the Old Testament, the Jewish Scriptures often reinforce much of Matthew's thought.

In preaching the magi narrative, I would make the following comments concerning the story's canonical-theological context. Matthew implicitly contrasts Jerusalem and Bethlehem. Jerusalem is the city of Herod and the religious elites who, like their ancestors before them, rejected God's servants sent to them (Matt 23:37–39) and have no regard for Jesus the infant king. Their indifference will escalate into full-blown rejection and the murder of Jesus (16:21; 20:17–18; 26–27). Bethlehem, by stark contrast, is the city of Jesus the Messiah, whose birth brings the visit of priestly gentile royals to pay him homage, echoing 1 Kings 10 (the queen of Sheba coming to King Solomon) and the eschatological fulfillment of Isaiah 60:6. The two Scripture texts cited in the story extol Jesus's greatness. Micah 5:2 speaks of Bethlehem being least despite its association with King David, but now because of its connection to Jesus it can no longer be considered least. Second Samuel 5:2

reveals both the Israel-first ethos of Jesus's messianic mission and the Davidic, messianic Shepherd character of his coming to the Jewish nation.

DANIEL 9:1-19

After completing the previous exegetical steps, in looking outward to the rest of the canon, Daniel's prayer would first be put in conversation with the rest of the book of Daniel. The book introduces the audience to Daniel, a captive from the Babylonian exile (1:1–7). Chapters 1–8 take place during the Babylonian era while chapters 10–12 occur during the Persian era. The setting for Daniel's prayer is the Medo-Persian period (9:1), which means Daniel's prayer for the end of the exile and return to the promised land serves as the bridge between these two larger geographically contrasting sections of the book. While the other prophecies of Daniel look deep into the future, his prayer seeks divine action now. When Daniel prays, he customarily prays three times per day, on his knees by an open window, facing Jerusalem (6:10). In direct response to Daniel's intercession for Jerusalem (9:1–19), an angel declares that Jerusalem will be rebuilt and restored (9:25). Thus, God will indeed answer Daniel's request.

The most organic canonical connections to Daniel's prayer are the Scripture texts he appeals to. He explicitly references Jeremiah's prophecy in 9:2 (Jer 29:10–14). Jeremiah's own prophetic ministry began before the Babylonian exile and extended into the exilic period. Jeremiah 29 represents the letter he wrote from Jerusalem to the Jews who survived the destruction of Jerusalem and who live in exile (Jer 29:1). The prophet encourages the exiles to settle down in Babylon and seek the nation's peace and prosperity, knowing that there will come a day—after seventy years of exile—when Yahweh will bring them back from their captivity to the land (Jer 29:10). This text inspires Daniel to offer the penitential prayer that he does in Daniel 9. Jeremiah did not live long enough to see the fulfillment of his prophecy, but Daniel did. He understood where he and the exiles stood in relation to God's prophetic program, and he prayed accordingly. Thus, we get a window into how Daniel reads and interprets prophecy. Another text organically linked to his prayer is Solomon's prayer of dedication for the Jerusalem temple in 1 Kings 8. The opening lines of Daniel's prayer implicitly cite 1 Kings 8:23 and 47, and the prayer closes by implicitly quoting 1 Kings 8:39. It is both ironic and appropriate that Daniel employs a prayer reserved for the inauguration of the temple: in seeking Jerusalem's restoration, he is praying for a new beginning for the temple *ipso facto*. And while Solomon could only anticipate from a distance a situation where the Jews would become captives in a foreign land, instructing them to face Jerusalem and repent of their sins (1 Kgs 8:46–51), that hypothetical scenario for Solomon becomes Daniel's reality. Here we observe an instance of Old Testament Scripture appropriating Old Testament Scripture for the purpose of fulfilment and application.

Daniel's penitential prayer falls into a class of similar prayers that it would be helpful to examine: Ezra 9 and Nehemiah 9. In the case of Ezra 9, despite taking place in the post-exilic period, like Daniel 9, the prayer is offered by someone labeled as an "exile" (Ezra 8:35; 10:8). Unlike the occasion for Daniel's prayer, Ezra launches into his intercession because of the intermarriage and religious intermingling between Jews and the surrounding gentile nations. In the prayer of Ezra 9, Ezra acknowledges his people's (i.e., the exiles' [9:4]) sin, guilt, and shame, confessing their failure to heed the words of the prophets, and thus, the people have justly reaped God's punishment. Both prayers are offered on account of Jerusalem, but for different reasons: for Daniel, it is because it lies in ruins; for Ezra, it is because God has granted the nation new life to rebuild the temple and he has enabled them to build a wall to protect Jerusalem from the nations. Unlike Daniel, who appears to be the lone intercessor, in response to Ezra's prayer the people confess their sins and consequently jettison their foreign wives. Daniel's intercession represents an individualized, pray-wait-and-watch perspective, whereas Ezra's resembles more of a corporate, pray-and-work attitude. According to Nehemiah 9, a small band of Levites offer the intercessory prayer (Neh 9:5). Their prayer is part of a solemn assembly revolving around the public reading of the Book of the Law. This prayer stands apart from Ezra's (and Daniel's) because most of it represents a retelling of salvation history, outlining how God acted graciously toward Israel and how the people refused to listen to God's prophets. Consequently, despite living in the land, they see themselves as slaves under oppressive leadership. The prayer results in a renewed commitment to follow God's law, to marry Jewish wives, and to care diligently for the operation of the Jerusalem temple. Ironically, Daniel had prayed for freedom from oppression, but a generation later, the people were "free" yet still oppressed.

Spiraling out beyond the Old Testament to the prayers in the New Testament yields further theological insights. Perhaps the most obvious prayer of comparison would be Jesus's high priestly prayer in John 17. The occasion for Jesus's prayer is that the time for his passion has come. He acknowledges his exclusive place in God's program of salvation, how he uniquely reveals God's glory, and how he receives and has kept God's gift of his eleven disciples. He asks God to preserve and sanctify them, as well as the next generation of believers, in the world. He also prays that believers would be unified, thereby reflecting the unity and glory that exists between the Father and the Son, and, ultimately, that his followers might be with Jesus again to behold his glory and to know, love, and to live in union with God. Jesus's prayer in some respects represents a prayer of consecration before his passion. The obvious contrast between Daniel's prayer and Jesus's lies in their respective realms of focus. Daniel's sights are set squarely on the earthly, geopolitical realm, while Jesus's intercession focuses on the spiritual realm. One similarity might be that both petitions show concern for the divine program of God's presence being with his people: in Jerusalem for Daniel and in Jesus (and then the church) for Jesus.

Daniel's prayer can also be put into conversation with the early church's prayer in Acts 4:24–31. The disciples offer their prayer in response to the persecution they suffer at the hands of the religious leaders. They begin by acknowledging God as the creator of all things; then they cite the prophetic words of David in Psalm 2 about the rulers of the nations raging and conspiring against God and against his Christ. In their prayer they see Psalm 2:1–2 as coming to its ultimate theological climax in the evil deeds done by Herod and Pontius Pilate to Jesus, in complete accord with God's sovereign will. Therefore, the church asks God to enable them to preach boldly and to perform signs and wonders through the name of Jesus. As a result of their intercession, the place where they are gathered shakes, they are filled with the Holy Spirit, and they preach the word of God boldly. Both Daniel and the early church presuppose God's sovereign rule over the nations. But while Daniel petitions God to release his people from their earthly bondage, the apostolic church asks him to enable them to preach and to bear witness despite living in the midst of religious and political persecution.

Paul's prayers could also serve as conversation partners. In Colossians 1:9–12, for example, the occasion for the apostle's intercession is his recounting of how he gives thanks for the Colossians' devoted witness: their faithfulness, fruitfulness, and hospitality. This statement of thanksgiving, consequently, leads him to pray for them. He asks God that they be filled with spiritual wisdom so that they can continue to please the Lord, being strengthened by him and giving thanks to God. Like Jesus's, Paul's prayer contrasts with Daniel's in regard to its distinctly spiritual emphasis; and, in fact, it is prompted not by crisis, like Daniel's, but by personal elation for the faithful witness of his Colossian brothers and sisters in their community.

When preaching Daniel's intercessory prayer, the first connection I would note is how it functions within the book. It serves as a bridge between the Babylonian exile of chapters 1–8 and the post-exilic return to the land in chapters 10–12. By placing this prayer as a fulcrum between these two large units, the author elevates the importance of penitential prayer for the people of God. As the rest of Scripture attests, God uses the prayers of his people to accomplish his sovereign purposes in their lives. Second, Daniel offers his intercession in light of Jeremiah 29:1–10. While God used the exile to chastise his people, Jeremiah's prophetic word to them was to settle down in Babylon and seek the nation's peace and prosperity. But this was only for a time, because God always planned to bring them back to their land (29:11–14). Prior to his prayer, Daniel had done exactly that: he had settled down in Babylon and sought and worked toward the nation's prosperity. But according to Jeremiah's prophecy, the time had come for him to work—through penitential prayer—for something else: his people's freedom.

ISAIAH 29:13-16

In looking outward to the rest of the canon, this passage would first be put into conversation with the rest of Isaiah. The oracle in 29:13-16 begins with the charge of ritualistic worship. The prophecy opens with a series of indictments against the people of God, including empty, formalistic worship (1:11-16), and cycles back to this charge in chapter 58, where Yahweh chastises his people for their hypocritical "observance" of fasting. Because of his people's vain worship, Yahweh promises to overturn their worldly standards and sensibilities: "The wisdom of the wise will perish, the intelligence of the intelligent will vanish" (29:14 NIV). The people of God thought themselves to be wise but instead were proud and arrogant—attitudes that the prophet regularly exposes and attacks (e.g., 2:11-12; 3:16; 5:15; 9:9; 28:1). The "woe" of judgment Isaiah proclaims in 29:15 echoes the previous woes he pronounced (29:1; cf. 5:8, 11, 19, 20-22; 6:5; 10:1, 5; *passim*). The prophet reminds his people that Yahweh is the sovereign potter who owes Israel, the clay, absolutely nothing; nor does Israel even have the right to judge God's sovereign ways. This theme of God's sovereignty, often intertwined with judgment, runs throughout the book of Isaiah. For example, when Isaiah speaks of God judging his people through the agency of the Assyrians, the will and actions of the two are conflated: God acts through the Assyrians to chastise Israel, yet from Assyria's perspective their conquering of Israel stems simply from their striving for global dominance—a hubris that leads to their punishment (10:5-15).

Spiraling out to the rest of the Old Testament, these Isaianic motifs appear and are further amplified elsewhere. Empty formalism is a definite theme in Jeremiah. Judah, for example, believes that the Jerusalem temple will serve as a buffer in the day of God's judgment against their overtly sinful ways (Jer 7:1-15). The core issue is their sinful, uncircumcised hearts (Jer 9:26), something God promises to rectify by giving his people a new heart (24:7; cf. 31:33). Perhaps the ultimate reversal of standards is evidenced in Jeremiah's prophecy of the new covenant: God's law will be written on the hearts of his people and, consequently, they will all know him personally and will no longer need a priestly or prophetic mediator as in times past (31:31-34). Isaiah's language of the potter and the clay finds a strong echo in Jeremiah 18-19. In Isaiah, the imagery has to do with depicting God's total mastery over his people in general. In Jeremiah, the imagery receives further specificity: God promises to raise up a foreign nation (Babylon) to chastise his people (Judah and Jerusalem) because of their sinful rebellion.

Spiraling out still further, the apostle Paul appropriates this potter-clay imagery in Romans 9, implicitly citing Isaiah 29:16. Whereas Isaiah applies the metaphor to the earthly realm, Paul ties it to God's absolute freedom in the sovereign election of individuals in salvation. The apostle also cites Isaiah 29:14 in 1 Corinthians 1:19 in his exposition of God's plan of salvation: in the cross God has maximally overturned and reversed conventional human wisdom. Jesus also quotes Isaiah 29. When rebuking the pharisees and teachers of the law regarding the distinction between clean and unclean, he tells them that Isaiah was prophesying against them (Matt 15:7-8; cf. Isa 29:13): the religious leaders were using their human-made traditions to negate the keeping of God's law. Thus, the issue of empty obedience in Isaiah's day continued to exist in Jesus's.

While Isaiah opines about how God, in dealing with his earthly people and the nations, will reverse human sensibilities, the greatest reversal for all times comes in the incarnation: Paul says that although Jesus was God, he became a slave and died on the cross (Phil 2:6–8), and that God appointed Jesus, who was sinless, to be sin for us (2 Cor 5:21); John proclaims that the eternal Word became flesh and lived among us (John 1:14); Jesus declares that the Son of Man (who will come in the clouds in the last day to judge the nations [Matt 25:31–32]) did not come to be served but to serve and give his life up as a ransom for many (Matt 20:28).

One obvious theological connection I would make for a sermon on this text would be to connect it to its use in the New Testament. Jesus refers to Isaiah 29:13 to make the point that the strict keeping of human (and not divine) legal traditions in Isaiah's day corresponds to the Jesus-rejecting, tradition-for-law observance of some of the Pharisees during the time of Jesus and his followers. In making this link Jesus demonstrates that God values the inner attitudes of the heart more than empty, external conformity to earthly standards. Another connection would be this: Paul cites Isaiah 29:16 in Romans 9. The divine sovereignty of God over the nations that echoes throughout the book of Isaiah comes to its fullest expression, according to Paul, in the doctrine of election. God, as the potter, not only has the right to intervene in the affairs of nations (evident in Isaiah), but he also has the right to choose some individuals for salvation while passing over others.

CONCLUSION

To follow Paul's counsel to his young protégé Timothy, "Do your best to present yourself to God as one approved, a worker who does not need to be ashamed and who correctly handles the word of truth" (2 Tim 3:15), you must bring the sermon text into conversation with other biblical passages to expand the theological and biblical horizons of your congregation in order to help foster greater theological and biblical maturity, thereby enabling them to "grow in the grace and knowledge of [the] Lord and Savior Jesus Christ" (2 Pet 3:18). Your conversation partners must be organic and not forced; they must emanate from the passage itself: for example, the passage cites or alludes to an Old Testament text(s), or it is conceptually connected, corresponding with a common biblical theme or motif. When theologically reflecting across the breadth of the canon, you need to be careful not to read meaning from other passages into your sermon text. Other passages can illumine the text, perhaps bringing out certain nuances, or amplify or illustrate what is already there. But other Bible passages should not be used to define the meaning of the text. Context remains the final determinant of meaning. Nor should you use other passages as a vehicle for reading out of the sermon text a full-blown canonical theology. For example, do not read into an Old Testament text all that we know post-Calvary, as if to imply that the Old Testament authors knew and wrote as we now know this side of the incarnation (this would overturn the idea of progressive revelation in the Bible). That is not to say that you can't preach the gospel from an Old Testament passage. You certainly can. But it only points forward in a veiled way to Christ. Only with the teaching of the New Testament does it receive clarity. For example, in the "Protoevangelium" of Genesis 3:15 ("I will put enmity between you and the woman, and between your offspring and her offspring; he shall bruise your head, and you shall bruise his heel"), the gospel is only presented in seed form. It does not proclaim the identity of the woman's offspring, nor does it declare how exactly he will crush the serpent's head. These all-important details only come from the New Testament. This verse points from a distance to the person and work of Christ; and insofar as it does, you can use it as a springboard for the gospel. In this way, you're not reading the gospel back into the text; rather, you're showing how the Old Testament passage foreshadows the gospel, and then preaching the gospel.

Examining the canonical context by connecting the sermon text with organic, biblical conversation partners would represent the penultimate stage in preparing a sermon from the page to the pulpit. The first six steps answer the question, So what? These chapters combine to demonstrate why the text is important. They do not, however, answer the question, Now what? The answer to this question represents the final stage of the process, to which we now turn.

RESOURCES

Fowl, S. *Engaging Scripture: A Model for Theological Interpretation.* Challenges in Contemporary Theology. Oxford: Blackwell, 1998.

Gorman, M. *Elements of Biblical Exegesis: A Basic Guide for Students and Ministers.* 3rd ed. Grand Rapids: Baker Academic, 2020.

Greidanus, S. *The Modern Preacher and the Ancient Text: Interpreting and Preaching Biblical Literature.* Grand Rapids: Eerdmans, 1989.

Kaiser, W. *Toward an Exegetical Theology: Biblical Exegesis for Preaching and Teaching.* Grand Rapids: Baker, 1981.

Osborne, G. *The Hermeneutical Spiral: A Comprehensive Introduction to Biblical Interpretation.* 2nd ed. Downers Grove, IL: IVP, 2006.

Sarisky, D. *Reading the Bible Theologically.* Current Issues in Theology. Cambridge: Cambridge University Press, 2019.

Tate, R. *Biblical Interpretation: An Integrated Approach.* 3rd ed. Grand Rapids: Baker Academic, 2008.

CHAPTER 8

BECOMING DOERS

APPLYING THE TEXT APPROPRIATELY

WE USE THEM daily, but we don't often think about the concept of roads. Author Jim Forest describes them like this:

> From times long before the written word, roads have linked house to house, town to town, and city to city. Without roads there are no communities. Roads not only connect towns but give birth to them. … The road is an invitation to cross frontiers, to start a dialogue, to end enmity. Each road gives witness to the need we have to be in touch with one another. … Roads are life giving.[1]

Preaching is like a journey along a life-giving road. The preacher is the tour guide who takes the audience, by way of an expository sermon, to a specific destination: a sanctifying encounter with the God of the Bible. Two intertwined elements comprise

---

1. Jim Forest, *The Road to Emmaus: Pilgrimage as a Way of Life* (Maryknoll, NY: Orbis Books, 2007), 1–2.

this holy encounter. The first has to do with knowing God. The sermon ought to move the listener to a deeper knowledge and understanding (both head and heart) of God through Jesus Christ. This kind of knowing leads to the second dimension of the encounter. When a sermon moves the hearers to a more intimate knowledge of God, this engenders within the audience a desire for faithful obedience to the Holy Spirit toward greater personal Christlikeness. The end of the homiletical path, then, is application: how to live in Christlike obedience to God.

Some people have argued against the notion of sermon application, believing that the gap it presupposes between the biblical text and the modern audience implies that the Bible lacks relevance, and it needs to be made relevant to us today.[2] Others contend that application is solely the job of the Holy Spirit, as John MacArthur trumpets: "When Scripture is accurately interpreted and powerfully preached, the Spirit takes the message and applies it to the particular needs of each listener."[3] Application for some preachers, then, is nothing more than an unnecessary add-on to the proclamation of Scripture. But as Sidney Greidanus rightly observes, "Since the message was first addressed to the ancient church, it requires explication; since that message now needs to be addressed to a contemporary church, it requires application."[4] What an ancient text says is not necessarily what it means today.

---

2. See, for example, Gary Findley, "Review of Bryan Chapell, *Christ-Centered Preaching: Redeeming the Expository Sermon*," *Kerux* 11 (May 1996), 37–41.

3. John MacArthur Jr., "Moving from Exegesis to Exposition," in *Rediscovering Expository Preaching*, ed. Richard Mayhew (Dallas: Word, 1992), 300. While this is true, the Holy Spirit often works through natural means. Just as God uses the means of prayer to direct and accomplish his sovereign purposes, so too the Spirit uses sermon application as a means of transforming the lives of his people.

4. Sidney Greidanus, *The Modern Preacher and the Ancient Text: Interpreting and Preaching Biblical Literature* (Grand Rapids, MI: Eerdmans, 1989), 183.

There is clear biblical warrant for application in preaching. The book of Acts provides obvious instances of this. At the end of Peter's sermon in Jerusalem on the day of Pentecost, for example, the crowd responds to his message with a question: What should we do? Peter has just explained to them the speaking in tongues phenomenon with a text from Joel 2. He testifies using the Psalms that Jesus of Nazareth is Lord and Messiah, and though the authorities crucified Jesus, God raised him from the dead. These are huge biblical and theological issues for any Jew that beg further reflection. Yet, their question to Peter is not theoretical ("How can these things be?"). It is, rather, both personal ("we") and practical ("do"). So, Peter caps off his sermon with application: Repent, be baptized (Acts 2:38), be saved (Acts 2:40). These are very concrete points of application. Knowing and believing the truth invariably leads to doing it.[5] Besides behavior, this "doing" of the truth entails things like attitudes, speech, values, beliefs, and personal identity. The apostle Paul, for his part, explains to Timothy the ultimate purpose of Scripture: "All Scripture is God-breathed and is useful for teaching, rebuking, correcting and training in righteousness, so that the servant of God may be thoroughly equipped for every good work" (2 Tim 3:16–17; cf. Rom 15:4). The activities that Paul describes—teaching, rebuking, correcting, and training—are very specific and not just general. Therefore, when we offer application in our sermons, we stand in a long homiletical tradition. The question, then, is not if, but how: How do we apply a passage?

---

5. According to Scripture, the truth is not something merely to be known. Truth is something to practice. For example, see 1 John 1:6: "If we say we have fellowship with him while we walk in darkness, we lie and do not *practice the truth*" (ESV, emphasis added cf. John 3:21).

Applying a text is not always simple. Haddon Robinson quips, "More heresy is preached in application than in Bible exegesis."[6] But heresy is not the only concern. Preachers often apply biblical texts sideways: they offer something generally true but not derived from the specific text being preached. Robinson observes that the long-term effect of this kind of application is the preaching of mythology: "Myth has an element of truth along with a great deal of puff, and people tend to live in the puff. They live with the implications of implications, and then discover that what they thought God promised, he didn't promise."[7]

When it comes to making application, the most common way to apply the text is to carry it straight over into the modern setting. Sometimes this works. For example, when Jesus exhorts his first-century Jewish audience to "Love your enemies and pray for those who persecute you" (Matt 5:44), that command likewise works well for a twenty-first-century Western audience. Similarly, injunctions prohibiting sexual immorality (like 1 Cor 6:18) remain immediately relevant today. However, this straightforward applicational transference can quickly run into problems. Jesus, for example, in response to the rich young ruler's question about inheriting eternal life, tells him to sell all his possessions and give the proceeds to the poor. Does this mean that Jesus demands every Christian to follow suit? If that were true, then the rest of the New Testament would contradict this notion.[8]

---

6. Haddon Robinson, "Is Application Necessary in the Expository Sermon?" in *The Art and Craft of Biblical Preaching: A Comprehensive Resource for Today's Communicators*, ed. Haddon Robinson and Craig Larson (Grand Rapids, MI: Zondervan, 2005), 306.

7. Robinson, "Is Application Necessary," 307.

8. In Acts 5, for example, the sin of Ananias was not that he failed to give all the money from his property sale to the apostles. It was, rather, that he offered them some of the proceeds but wanted them to think that it was the full amount. Indeed, Peter

For Philippians 2:6–11, a direct correspondence between the text and the modern audience might look like this:

In light of this passage, we must:

- Become a servant like Jesus.

- Be willing to die for others like Jesus.

- Expect to be exalted like Jesus.

These points of application would not be entirely wrong. After all, they seem to emerge from the text, and they also align with broader biblical truth. Nevertheless, I think they lose some of their proclamational power because they do not mirror the thrust of Paul's teaching in the passage. Rather than traveling directly forward into the heart of the listener, these application points drift sideways, softening their impact on the hearer.

Applying a biblical text appropriately involves a number of important considerations. First, in your exegesis you need to determine the purpose or point of the passage. What function does it have in the book? Bryan Chapell argues that for application to be most effective it must be in line with a text's priorities.[9] This is where "Discerning the Big Picture" (chapter 3) becomes even more crucial. Assessing the co-text will help you answer the question of a text's purpose. As we saw earlier in Philippians 2:6–11, the majestic Christ Hymn serves a very specific purpose in the flow of Paul's thought in the letter: to illustrate for the church the kind of attitude they need to embrace in order to help them navigate their interpersonal

---

told him, "Didn't [the proceeds] belong to you before it was sold? And after it was sold, wasn't the money at your disposal?" (Acts 5:4) There is no divine or apostolic edict for believers to sell all their possessions. Examples like this one could be multiplied.

9. Bryan Chapell, *Christ-Centered Preaching: Redeeming the Expository Sermon*, 2nd ed. (Grand Rapids, MI: Baker Academic, 2005), 212.

conflicts better. Knowing that this is how the passage functions in its context enables you to draw more accurate and appropriate points of application for your audience. More precise and directed application from Philippians 2:6–11 would fall along these lines:

In light of this passage:

- When we find ourselves in conflict, we need to walk in a posture of humility, whereby we refrain from using our privileges and entitlements for personal gain.

- Serving others means using the privileges or entitlements we might have to build up our brothers and sisters even in the midst of conflict.

- When we follow Jesus in this way, we can expect God to reward us at the second coming.

Second, appropriate application follows when we make ourselves aware of the original audience. As moderns we stand in a massive interpretive gap created by the enormous differences of time, language, and cultural norms, as well as differences in shared experiences between ourselves and the original audience. Therefore, application that assumes a straightforward, one-to-one correspondence between the text and the modern hearer frequently misses the target. When lecturing about the need to study the social-historical background of a biblical text, I sometimes tell my class (tongue-in-cheek) that the toughest temptation for me to withstand is the urge to disobey God's commandment in Exodus 23:19: "Do not cook a young goat in its mother's milk" (NIV). Daily I walk into my kitchen at home and struggle mightily trying to resist the siren's enticing whispers to violate this command. Clearly, direct application is out of the question: it doesn't work. Is there a way to apply this verse to a modern reader? Yes, by understanding the original audience in their social-historical context. Exodus scholars argue for one of two possible cultural aspects underlying this prohibition. One is that the Canaanites would cook a kid in its mother's milk as a way of appeasing the gods of fertility. The other option is that the law forbids the commingling of what would represent the forces of life and the forces of death. Either way, this law represents one of the means by which the Israelites were to differentiate themselves from their pagan neighbors in their worship of Yahweh. And therein lies the key for applying this text appropriately today. Christians must not try to worship God the way other groups worship their gods: by legalistic ritual, by paying little or no attention to morality or ethics, or by adopting the traditions and practices of other religions.

Third, appropriate application means you need to be aware of the audience to whom you're preaching: their demographic makeup and their needs. The demographics of the original audience was far different than any Western modern audience. While the original hearers would have readily recognized how the message applied—since it originated in their own time and setting—this is less obvious for people listening today in a very different social context. Daniel, for example, intercedes in Daniel 9:1–19 for his fellow Jewish exiles hoping for the end of the Babylonian exile and the restoration of Israel to their land. His contemporaries, as well as later generations of Jews who found themselves under Greek and then Roman oppression, could easily pray this prayer as written. But what about us today? The Western church is not in geopolitical exile, nor are we a political entity in the world. The Western church, however, lives in sociocultural exile. We no longer occupy the center of our society.[10] Thus, one way to apply Daniel's prayer as a whole in our modern context would be to use it to pray for the church's release from sociocultural exile/marginalization.

Fourth, making appropriate application means that you need to keep real people in mind as you write your sermon. Returning to Philippians 2:6–11, the broad-stroke points of application outlined above should be narrowed to reflect specific types of people and situations. For example:

GENERAL APPLICATION	SPECIFIC APPLICATION
When we find ourselves in conflict, we need to walk in a posture of humility, whereby we refrain from using our privileges and entitlements for personal gain.	An "A" student in school could use his/her designated study time to help a student struggling in the same course. A stellar athlete could devote some practice time to helping a less-talented teammate. People could use their hard-earned bonus money to help out someone less fortunate than themselves.

<hr>

10. See W. Baxter, *We've Lost. What Now? Practical Counsel from the Book of Daniel* (Eugene, OR: Wipf & Stock, 2015), xi–xiv, 1–7.

GENERAL APPLICATION	SPECIFIC APPLICATION
Serving others means using the privileges or entitlements we might have to build up our brothers and sisters even in the midst of conflict.	For those who love to write, send encouraging notes to someone with whom you disagree on a personal matter. For those with gifts in hospitality, use that gift to build up a brother or sister with whom you're experiencing a relational impasse. For prayer warriors, write out and send an encouraging intercessory prayer to the other person ("My prayer for you is …").
When we follow Jesus in this way, we can expect God to reward us at the second coming.	Whenever we follow Jesus in this way, we don't need to hope for the commendation of other people; we don't need to desire the admiration of those we serve; we don't even need to look for a "thank you for your service." When we don't receive any kind of recognition, we need not become offended or stew in our anger because we know that we will receive much higher and far more satisfying praise from God when Jesus returns.

By applying the biblical text appropriately, then, sermon application, in conjunction with the rest of the sermon, should answer two questions: So what? (Why is this passage important to me?) And now what? (What should I do about it?)[11]

CONCLUSION

The destination of the journey of preaching is a sanctifying encounter with the God of the Bible. The life-giving road of expository preaching starts in the sacred pages of Scripture and extends into the modern human experience. Pastor Louis Lotz aptly describes the journey-destination like this:

> Good preaching begins in the Bible, but it doesn't stay there. It visits the hospital and the college dorm, the factory and the farm, the kitchen and the office, the bedroom and the classroom. ... Good preaching invades the real world, and it talks to real people—the high-school senior who's there because he's dragged there; the housewife who wants a divorce; the grandfather who mourns the irreversibility of time and lives with a frantic sense that almost all the sand in the hourglass has dropped; the farmer who is about to lose his farm, the banker who must take it from him.[12]

Because the Bible is God's word to us and it speaks with divine authority, it makes demands on the hearer. Sometimes the demand is explicit: "Share with the Lord's people who are in need. Practice hospitality" (Rom 12:13). Sometimes it is implicit. But the demand to follow God is always there in the Scriptures. Our job as preachers is to help our people identify the demand

---

11. David Veerman, "Sermons: Apply Within," *Leadership* (Spring 1990), 122.

12. Louis Lotz, "Good Preaching," *Reformed Review* 40 (Autumn 1986), 38.

God is revealing to them through the sermon so they can reach the destination of greater Christlikeness in their sanctifying encounter with the Living God.

RESOURCES

Bettler, John. "Application." Pages 331–49 in *The Preacher and Preaching*. Edited by Samuel Logan. Phillipsburg, NJ: Presbyterian and Reformed Publishing, 1986.

Chapell, Bryan. *Christ-Centered Preaching: Redeeming the Expository Sermon*. 2nd edition. Grand Rapids, MI: Baker Academic, 2005.

Greidanus, Sidney. *The Modern Preacher and the Ancient Text: Interpreting and Preaching Biblical Literature*. Grand Rapids: Eerdmans, 1989.

Robinson, Haddon, and Craig Larson, eds. *The Art and Craft of Biblical Preaching: A Comprehensive Resource for Today's Communicators*. Grand Rapids, MI: Zondervan, 2005.

York, Hershael, and Scott Blue. "Is Application Necessary in the Expository Sermon?" *The Southern Baptist Journal of Theology* 3/2 (1999): 70–84.

CHAPTER 9

CONCLUSION

A SERMON REVISITED

IN THE INTRODUCTION, I described a sermon on Jesus's baptism in Matthew 3:13–17 that I preached as a young layperson. At the time, I offered what I thought was a solid, verse-by-verse exposition of the passage, with my points being:

1. We need to live obediently. (v. 13)

2. Sometimes people in the church won't understand our attempts to obey God. (v. 14)

3. We must always strive to obey God more than we obey people. (v. 15)

4. We can expect God's blessing whenever we obey him. (vv. 16–17)

Again, my points were biblically sound and theologically true, but they were not rooted in the passage itself—the opposite of genuine expository preaching, which "exposits" or "exposes" the author's message in a given text. How would I approach this passage today?

Well, Matthew 3:13–17 is a complete unit of thought, so I did get that right (see chapter 2, "Keeping It Together"). But after that, the exegetical process diverged sharply from what I would later learn. To begin with, I never sought to integrate Matthew's baptismal account into its wider literary context of Matthew 1:1–4:11 (chapter 3, "Discerning the Big Picture"). It turns out that the co-text deeply informs the baptismal account. In the chapters leading up to the pericope, Matthew introduces Jesus in the birth and infancy traditions as the Messiah, the Christ. He is the Son of David, the Son of Abraham; he is conceived by the Holy Spirit; he is God with us ("Emmanuel"); he is the Davidic shepherd/ruler, who is worshiped by foreign nobility but despised by the Jewish leaders. Matthew 3 opens with John the Baptist, whom God has appointed to be the forerunner of the Messiah, to prepare the hearts of God's people to receive him. John baptizes people for the forgiveness of sins (3:6). Jesus's baptism by John, however, is not a matter of mere obedience like it was with the penitent Jews who sought John's baptism. At this point, my twenty-three-year-old self was offside.

Matthew scholars indicate that the words of God the Father from heaven (v. 17) allude to Psalm 2:7 and Isaiah 42:1[1] and thereby suggest that, by his baptism, Jesus identifies as God's Son and as God's Servant, that is, the Servant of Yahweh. Jesus's divine sonship has already been introduced in the narrative. On the one hand, because he is the rightful heir to David's throne (1:1–17), that makes Jesus, the Son of David, the Son of God by

---

1. See, for example, the commentaries of Donald Hagner (Word Biblical Commentary), Grant Osborne (Zondervan Exegetical Commentary on the New Testament), R. T. France (New International Commentary on the New Testament), and D. A. Carson (Expositor's Bible Commentary).

virtue of his kingship (2:2). On the other hand, his sonship is more than titular, it is essential, as 1:18–25 demonstrates: Jesus was conceived by the Holy Spirit and born of a virgin. The voice of God declaring Jesus's divine sonship merely makes explicit what is already implicit in the story.

The passage that immediately follows the baptism also reinforces Jesus's divine sonship. In Matthew 4:1–11 Matthew draws a typological comparison between Jesus and Israel. Yahweh called Israel his "firstborn son" (Exod 4:22–23); now God calls Jesus his "beloved son." God calls his son Israel out into the wilderness; the Holy Spirit leads Jesus out into the wilderness. Israel as God's son spent forty years in the wilderness experiencing testing (Deut 8); so too, Jesus, God's true Son, must spend forty days and forty nights in the wilderness to be tested by Satan.[2] Thus, Jesus's divine sonship, as declared by God at his baptism, anticipates the wilderness of testing, where his divine sonship will be typologically enacted. Clearly, when the co-text is considered, much more is afoot in the passage than what I originally had thought. How would I outline it now?

The first step would be a phrase diagram (chapter 4, "Outlining the Passage"). My twenty-three-year-old self did not know Greek, but the text can still be outlined in English using a literal translation (like the ESV, below) by placing the main clauses at the left margin and indenting the subordinate clauses:

> [13] Then Jesus came from Galilee to the Jordan to John,
>
>   to be baptized by him.

---

2. And both experienced the same categories of temptation: independence, presumption, and idolatry. That Jesus twice cites from Deuteronomy (8:3; 6:13) in the temptation story indicates his own self-conscious comparison with Israel.

¹⁴ John would have prevented him, saying,

> "I need to be baptized by you, and
> do you come to me?"

¹⁵ But Jesus answered him,

> "Let it be so now, for thus it is fitting for us to
> fulfill all righteousness."

Then he consented.

> ¹⁶ And when Jesus was baptized,

immediately he went up from the water,

and behold, the heavens were opened to him,

and he saw the Spirit of God

> descending like a dove and coming to rest
> on him;

¹⁷ and behold, a voice from heaven said,

> "This is my beloved Son, with whom
> I am well pleased."

Several things stand out from this outline. Although John the Baptist seems to be a major character in this scene, the outline suggests the opposite: he has only a minor role, particularly compared to Jesus and God: most of the pericope focuses on Jesus and God, that is, the Spirit and the Father; John disappears after verse 15. In fact, at Jesus's baptism in verse 16, John is not even mentioned, contrary to how Matthew mentioned him when John baptizes others (3:6).

There are three speeches in the passage, and although they are short, they are telling, for they heighten in terms of dramatic effect. John's speech reveals his misunderstanding of what God requires, as well as his diminutive status compared to Jesus. Jesus's speech reveals his superior status to John (he essentially commands John to baptize him) and his correct understanding of God's will. God the Father's speech confirms Jesus's messianic identity as Son and Servant—the very reason for Jesus's baptism—and reveals his full approval of Jesus and his mission, as well as his special relationship with Jesus. In terms of mapping Matthew 3:13–17 according to the essential elements of the story:

- Introduction: Jesus arrives from Galilee to where John was baptizing people.

- Rising action: Jesus asks John for baptism but John resists.

- Climax: Jesus is baptized, and the heavens open and the Spirit descends upon Jesus.

- Conclusion: God the Father speaks from heaven affirming Jesus's messianic identity.

Clearly, the central point of the account is not Jesus's baptism per se—unlike with repentant Israelites who received John's baptism—but what it brings forth: the Holy Spirit's coming upon Jesus and God's vocal approval of Jesus and the mission he is about to embark on. God's purpose for Jesus's baptism, then, was far different than it was for penitent Jews.

The meaning of Jesus's baptism, when understood in light of the pericope's inner movement (vv. 16–17) and especially when read within the co-text of 1:1–4:11, was, on the one hand, about him symbolically identifying as the true Israel, the true Son of God. A second reason Jesus submits to John's baptism is because he symbolically identifies as the Servant of the Lord (which gets amplified in Matthew 12:17–21, where Isaiah 42:1–4 is explicitly applied to Jesus). While God appointed Israel to be his servant, Jesus is the ultimate Servant of Yahweh, and this servanthood characterizes Jesus's messiahship (Matt 20:28). When John tries to deter Jesus from being baptized, it is not because he misunderstands Jesus's obedience to God but because he misunderstands God's program for Israel through Jesus.[3] Jesus, then, is not modeling that Christians must always strive to obey God more than people—although that truth is clearly taught elsewhere in Scripture (e.g., Acts 5:29). This passage is about how Jesus fulfilled God's ancient program for his people Israel. Thus, it does not conclude with the promise of blessing for those who obey God—although, again, that principle can be seen elsewhere in the Bible (e.g., Luke 14:11). The final verses of the text instead point us to Jesus's sacred identity as Son of God and Servant of Yahweh, which significantly shape the course of his ministry. The passage is ultimately not about us and our (goal of) obedience to God, but about Jesus and his obedience to his Father.

The exegetical summary outline, which groups together the main clauses (chapter 5, "The Outline Before the Outline"), would look like this:

1. Jesus comes from Galilee to the Jordan to John. (v. 13)

2. John tries to prevent Jesus from being baptized. (v. 14)

3. Jesus persuades John to do it. (v. 15)

4. Jesus goes up out of the water. (v. 16)

---

3. Cf. Matt 11:1–6, where the Baptist's misunderstanding of the divine program causes him to do an about-face and begin to doubt Jesus's messiahship.

5. The heavens were opened to him. (v. 16)

6. He sees the Spirit of God. (v. 16)

7. A voice from heaven speaks. (v. 17)

The first section of the text deals with Jesus and John's interaction; the second part treats the interaction between Jesus and God the Father. The corresponding homiletical outline, then, could look like:

1. Jesus came to accomplish the mission of God. (vv. 13–15)

2. The origin, power, and message of Jesus's mission is God. (vv. 16–17)

When compared to the original sermon, what immediately jumps out is the difference in orientation. My original message was very human-centered and application focused. Carefully considering the co-text as well as the structure and inner movement of the passage has transformed the sermon to become God-centered and kingdom (mission) focused.

When it comes to "managing the minutiae" (chapter 6), a number of things catch the eye. There appears to be one purpose clause and one result clause: Jesus came to John "*to be* baptized by him," i.e., for the purpose of receiving John's baptism; and Jesus placates John's protestations, saying, "Let it be so now, *for thus* it is fitting for us to fulfill all righteousness" (ESV). In other words, John baptizing Jesus will result in the fulfilling of God's righteousness. "Righteousness" would be the one theologically loaded word that would need some explanation, especially since it is both central to the pericope and is a prominent motif in Matthew's Gospel. The other word that

would need to be investigated because of its function in the
account and its major role in the Gospel as a whole is "fulfill."
In the story's climax (vv. 16–17), two things stand out. First, all
three members of the Trinity appear: Jesus the Son is baptized,
the Holy Spirit descends on him like a dove afterward, and
the Father by means of a voice from heaven proclaims his love
for the Son. Second, there seems to be a contrast in verse 16
between Jesus going up from the water and the Spirit coming
down from heaven. Several different things may be at play in
this contrast. Jesus's obedience in baptism directly results in
him being given the Spirit. Water baptism is an earthly rite,
whereas the Spirit is heavenly. Jesus's earthly obedience leads to
heavenly activity on his behalf. So, it is possible that the double
linking of "behold" with "heaven" ("*behold*, the *heavens* were
opened to him" and "*behold*, a voice from *heaven*" affirms him)
emphasizes this point. I did not know any Greek back in the
day, but those are significant observations that a close reading
of the text in translation can produce.

Now, however, I do read Greek, and therefore it would
behoove me to assess the minutiae of the passage in its original
language rather than merely depending on an English translation.[4] Valuable nuances stand out in the Greek text, but only
three of which I will point out. First, in verse 13, the genitive
article affixed to the infinitive (τοῦ βαπτισθῆναι) indicates purpose, meaning Jesus came to John for the purpose of being
baptized by him, thus signifying the importance of the trans-
action that was about to transpire between them. Second, in
verse 14, when John tries to "prevent" (διεκώλυεν) Jesus from
being baptized, the imperfect tense means that there was a

---

4. The outline of the passage in Greek matches closely with the English, so there
is no need to repeat it here.

bit of a back and forth going on. In other words, John did not simply say "No" to Jesus: he likely kept insisting that Jesus not subject himself to his baptism, probably offering all kinds of reasons why he could not do what Jesus was asking him to do. Third, in the final verse of the pericope, when God declares "This is my beloved Son," "this" (οὖτός) is fronted for emphasis: in other words, as hallowed a prophet as John was— "among those born of women there has not risen anyone greater than John the Baptist" (Matt 11:11 ESV)—only Jesus and not John nor anyone in the crowds standing there was God's beloved Son (cf. Matt 17:4–5).

Applying chapter 7 ("Making Theological Connections"), the most obvious conversation partners for Matthew 3:13–17 are the two texts alluded to: Psalm 2:7 and Isaiah 42:1. What do these two texts mean in their original contexts, respectively? Does Matthew modify them, and how? There would be other conversation partners. The pericope occurs in the other Gospels. Mark's shorter version downplays the interaction between Jesus and John. Luke, too, downplays this dynamic and also splits up the temptation narrative from the baptismal story with his genealogy. This difference suggests that Matthew seeks to emphasize Jesus as Israel more than the other Gospel writers do. John's Gospel reveals that the Baptist had no messianic self-consciousness, that is, he knew that he was not the Messiah and that someone else was (namely, Jesus). Another associated text would be Matthew's introduction of John in the immediately preceding pericope, Matthew 3:1–12. The Evangelist quotes Isaiah 40:3 in relation to John: as Isaiah prophesied the end of the Babylonian exile for ancient Israel, so too, John prophesies the end of the nation's spiritual exile because of the coming Christ, which Jesus's baptism serves to initiate.

Because the context of my original "sermon" was an adult Sunday school class, that setting would have provided ample opportunity to dig into these different scriptural conversations, with little need to leave anything behind on the cutting room floor of my study. In a sermon, however, with limited time and usually no opportunity for immediate dialogue with the congregation, incorporation into the message would be different, and most observations would not necessarily find their way into the pulpit. Nevertheless, some should—perhaps those texts most tightly connected to the passage. But regardless, making biblical and theological connections remains an important activity for preachers because it helps us not to lose sight of the grand metanarrative of Scripture of God working salvation for his people; and this kind of reflection serves to strengthen a congregation's overall grasp of the Bible.

Finally, while my original main points were framed in an applicative manner, I did not try to offer concrete application for my audience. Moreover, my points clearly drifted sideways from Matthew's purpose for this text. The overall point of the passage is not about obedient living; it is christological and missional: Jesus is the true Son of God and Servant of the Lord who has come to fulfill God's purposes. This thrust, then, leads to the homiletical outline:

1. Jesus came to accomplish the mission of God.

2. The origin, power, and message of Jesus's mission is God.

Each of these points would need to be directly applied to my audience, which at the time consisted of a dozen people, mostly married couples between forty and seventy years of age, with one single, middle-aged man. How might I apply these truths to that group?

1. Jesus came to accomplish the mission of God.

   Application:

   a. Given how God's mission is lived out in the life of Jesus, what is the mission of God in your life?

   b. How can your marriage reflect more of the mission of God?

   c. How can your parenting/grandparenting reflect the mission of God?

   d. What about your career choices?

   e. How can the mission of God be reflected in your retirement?

   f. How can you use your singleness to reflect more of the mission of God?

   g. How can the mission of God be reflected during a time of loss?

2. The origin, power, and message of Jesus's mission is God

   Application:

   a. How does knowing that God is the origin, power, and message of Jesus's mission affect the way you think about Jesus? How does it affect the way you think about the other members of the Trinity?

b. How does knowing that the authority and power for you to live out God's mission comes from him help you carry it out?

c. What are things we do that short-circuit God's power and authority in our lives which inhibit us from seeing his mission carried out in/ through us?

d. What are things we can practice to experience more of God's authority and power to enable us to live out his mission more effectively?

THE SERMON ENVISIONED

In his book *The Challenge of Preaching*, John Stott writes:

> If we preach the Scriptures faithfully, the Holy Spirit will make the word of God live in the hearts of our hearers. Through his word God will give his people the vision without which the church will perish. First, they will begin to see that he wants his church to be his new society in the world. Then they will begin to grasp the resources he has given us in Christ to fulfil this purpose. Only by humble and obedient listening to his voice can the church grow to maturity, serve the world and glorify our Lord.[5]

Preaching is ultimately about God and his mission, not us. Since God has preserved his Word for us, and the central message of Scripture is God, it behooves any would-be Christian herald to proclaim Scripture so that God might be encountered in

---

5. John Stott, *The Challenge of Preaching*, abridged and updated by Greg Scharf (Grand Rapids: Eerdmans, 2015), 23.

the preaching of his word. One of the problems with a lot of so-called biblical preaching in churches today is that it offers only an exegetically lazy, humanistic vision of Jesus. Such lowly depictions of Christ from the pulpit only serve to obscure a congregation's view of who he really is. Yes, Jesus is the "friend of sinners." He is fully human, and, as the author of Hebrews tells us, Jesus can identify with all of our weaknesses, making him the perfect high priest. And for that we can be ever grateful!

Nevertheless, Jesus is the Christ, the Messiah. He is the Son of God in a way that no child of God can ever be. He is the Servant of the Lord in a way that no Christian can ever serve. He is the transcendent creator God, and there is no one like him! Christology affects everything: how we see God; how we see ourselves; how we view sin, Scripture, life, and death. A low, inadequate view of Jesus points us in a wrong and dangerous direction with each of these realities. A low Christology taxes our souls, sometimes without us even knowing it. But a high Christology—gazing at the Jesus of Scripture—is life-giving. Christocentric preaching, arrived at by a careful exegesis of the text, imparts to the audience this crucial, life-giving vision of Jesus.

The sad corollary to a humanistic vision of Jesus is Bible application apart from theological understanding. Pastors want to demonstrate to their flock the abiding relevance of ancient Scripture—that it can still apply to people's lives today. That's a good thing. The problem, however, is that the humanistic application that such a vision produces leads church members to, in the words of Haddon Robinson, "live in the puff." The process for drawing appropriate sermon application is not: "This is what the text says, therefore, this is what it means to me." This kind of faulty thinking leads to superficial not mature faith. Rather, the applicational move proceeds from: "This is what the text says," to "This is what it meant to the original author and audience," to "This is what it means for us today." Proper application of the Bible cannot happen apart from both biblical proclamation and a deeper theological understanding of Scripture. While there were many laws that the ancient Jews were responsible to keep, these laws were never "applied" apart from hearing and understanding the constant refrain: This is who the Lord God is; this is what the Lord God has done; therefore, this is what the Lord God will do for us. May God grant us this vision for the sermons we write and preach to his people.

SCRIPTURE INDEX

OLD TESTAMENT

Genesis

1:1 23
1:1–2:4a 33
1:3–5 73
1:31 23
2:4a 23, 24
2:4 27
2:4b 24
2:4b–25 33
2:15 111
2:24 121
3:14 111
3:15 154
4:1a 129
4:17a 129
4:25a 129
5:1 27
6:9 27
10:1 27
11:31–32 .... 24n1
12:1–3 .... 77, 106, 143
12:1–4 24
12:4–5 47
12:4–9 24
12:10–20 .... 24, 76
13:8–12 47
18:1–15 46

18:1–16 .... 35, 47
18:2 36
18:6 36
18:7 36
18:16–33 46
18:17 100
18:17–18 98
18:17–19 .... 101, 102
18:17–20 102
18:17–33 .... 35, 46, 47,
74, 98
18:20 100
18:20–21 .... 98, 101
18:22 .... 100, 101
18:22–23 98
18:22–32 101
18:22b–23a 102
18:23 100
18:23–32 .... 98, 102
18:23b–32 102
18:26 100
18:27 101
18:29 101
18:30 101
18:31 101
18:32 101
18:33 .... 98, 101, 102

19:1 36
19:1–29 36
19:16–26 75
19:27–29 75
19:29 47

Exodus

4:22–23 169
23:19 161

Numbers

27:17 144

Deuteronomy

6:13 .... 169n2
8:3 .... 169n2
32:5 138

Joshua

5:13–15 140

Judges

13:16–23 140

Ruth

3:13–22 143

1 Samuel

1:1–20 24

1:21–28 24
2:1–10 25
2:12–26 25
2:27–36.................... 25
15:23 111

2 Samuel
5:2 .... 142, 145
13:1 119
13:4 119
13:15 119

1 Kings
8:23 147
8:39 147
8:46–51................... 147
8:47......................... 147

Ezra
8:35 147
9:4........................... 147
10:8 147

Nehemiah
9:5 148

Job
1:1 44
1:2–3.........................44
1:5............................44
1:14–17......................44
1:18–19......................44
2:7–8.........................44
2:9............................44
2:11–13 45
3–37...........................45
38–41 45
42:1–2a 128
42:1–6 .... 44, 125, 127,
                         128

42:2 ....126, 127
42:3 ....126, 127
42:7–17 44

Psalms
2:1–2 149
2:7 ....168, 175
14:1............................21
23:1a...................... 108
23:1......................... 145
51:17 78
78:70–72...............144
95:1–7a 107
95:7b–11 107

Isaiah
1:11–16..................... 151
5:8 151
5:11 151
5:15.......................... 151
5:19.......................... 151
5:20–22.................... 151
6:5 151
9:9........................... 151
10:1.......................... 151
10:5.......................... 151
10:5–15 151
28:1 151
29:13................ 152, 153
29:13–14 25
29:13–16................... 151
29:14 ....151, 152
29:15........................ 151
29:16 .... 152, 153
40:11....................... 145
40–55 140
42:1.................168, 175
42:1–4 171
42:6.........................143
44:8.........................141

44–46 141
45:23 .... 139, 140
45:23b 141
54:1 26
60:6 .... 143, 145

Jeremiah
7:1–15 152
9:26.........................152
18–19 152
23:1–4 ....144, 145
24:7..........................152
29:1 146
29:1–10....................150
29:10 147
29:10–14 146
29:11–14 150
31:8–11 144
31:31–34 152
31:33 152

Ezekiel
34:11–16..................144

Daniel
1:1–7 146
1–8..................146, 150
2:1–45 49
2:46–47 48
2:47..........................49
2–4 49
3:1............................48
3:4–6 48
3:28a 49
3:29 50
4:2–3 49
6:10 146
7:13–14 140
9:1 146
9:1–19............. 146, 162

9:2 146
9:25 146
10–12 .... 146, 150

Micah
5:1 142
5:2 .... 142, 145

Zechariah
12:10–14 106

NEW TESTAMENT

Matthew
1:1 40
1:1–17 .... 36, 41, 142,
                          168
1:1–2:23 41
1:1–4:11 ...... 41, 168, 171
1:18a 94, 96
1:18 .... 71, 97
1:18b 96
1:18–19 97
1:18–25 .... 36, 41, 69, 71,
               94, 116, 169
1:19 .... 71, 94, 96, 97
1:20 .... 71, 94
1:20–21 .... 96, 97
1:20–25 97
1:21 142
1:22 .... 71, 94, 116
1:22–23 97
1:23–2:12 40
1:24 .... 71, 94, 96, 97
1:24–25 97
1:25a 115
1:25 .... 71, 94, 96, 97
1–2 41
2:1 144
2:1–12 ..... 24, 40, 41, 79,
                  141, 145
2:1–14 40
2:1–18 24
2:2 .... 36, 144, 169
2:3 144
2:13–18 24
2:13–23 .... 24, 41

2:16 145
2:19–23 24
3:1–12 175
3:1–4:11 41
3:5 141
3:6 .... 168, 170
3:13 .... 167, 172, 174
3:13–15 173
3:13–17 ..... 1, 3, 167, 168,
                  171, 175
3:14 .... 167, 172, 174
3:15 .... 167, 170, 172
3:16 .... 170, 172, 173
3:16–17 ...... 167, 171, 173,
                          174
3:17 .... 168, 173
4:1–11 169
4:23 37
4:23–9:35 142
4:25 141
5:3–12 3
5:16 37
5:20 123
5:21–48 123
5:35 141
5:44 159
5–7 37
8:22–23 .... 3n1
8–9 37
9:35 37
10:5–6 142
11:1–6 .... 172n3
11:11 175
11:29 139

12:17–21 171
15:7–8 152
16:14 126
16:21 .... 141, 145
16:24 .... 3n1
17:4–5 175
20:17–18 .... 141, 145
20:28 .... 139, 153, 172
21:12–20 141
22:41–46 144
22:45 144
23:37–39 .... 141, 145
24:22 122
25:31–32 153
25:31–34 144
25:31–46 139
26–27 145
27:37 144
27:42 144
27:53 141
28:19 142

Mark
6:34 144
12:29 130
16:1 69
16:1–8 69
16:2 69
16:3 .... 69, 114
16:4 69
16:5 69
16:6 115
16:8 .... 69, 70

Luke

1:15–23 141
2:21–38 141
2:40 145
2:41 145
2:41–49......................141
14:11 172
24:47 ....141, 142
24:52–53...................141

John

1:1 108
1:1–5 139
1:1–14 23
1:14................... 122, 153
3:7 58
3:14–15......................60
3:16 60
3:17.....................59, 63
3:21..................... 158n5
6:63............................. 5
9:2 110
13–17 121
19:3..........................114

Acts

1:8...................141, 142
1:16–19 36
2:38 158
2:40 158
4:24–31 149
5:4..........................160n8
5:29 172
6:4..............................43
7:55 139
15:1–35 142

Romans

3:9 112
3:9b–12 ....112n9

3:21–22.............. 123n24
3:23 112
5:1............. 55, 57, 62, 63
5–8 ....78n16
6:1 28
6:2–11........................28
6:15 28
6:16–23 28
8:13 122
9:8..............................122
9–11 143
12:13 165
15:4 158

1 Corinthians

1:19 152
6:18 159
7:1a 27
7:1b–24 27
7:25a 27
7:25b–40 27
8:1a 27
10:10.........................137
12:1a 27
12–14......................... 27
15:23–28...................139
16:1a.......................... 27

2 Corinthians

5:21............................153
7:7–9......................... 106

Galatians

1:11.................... 27n3, 91
1:11–12 ....88, 92, 93
1:11–24 ....88, 92
1:13 91
1:13–14 92
1:13–16a 91
1:14............................ 91

1:15–24................ 91, 92
1:16b–23 94
1:17 91
1:17–21 88
1:18 91
1:19 91
1:21 91
1:22 91
1:23 91
1:23–24 94
1:24 91
2:20 118
3:1............................... 63
3:8–9...................... 143
3:16 143
4:1–7 ....81, 82
4:5 82
4:21–31 141
4:28 26
4:28–5:1.....................26
4:31...........................26
5:1.............................26
5:1b 26
5:2–15........................26

Ephesians

1:4–5 56
2:11–22..............26, 142
2:13–15 43
3:1–13 ....26, 43
3:8 43
3:14 43
3:14–15.............. 41, 110
3:14–19 68
3:14–21...............26, 41
3:16 110
3:16–19...............41, 68
3:16–21 41
3:20–21 41
4:11 144

5:15–25 27
5:18 137
5:22 27
5:25 28

Philippians

1:1–2 22
1:1–11 39
1:3 68
1:3–4 .... 125n28
1:3–8 22
1:3–11 .... 65, 68
1:4–8 68
1:5 .... 125n30
1:6 .... 113, 116,
                    125n30
1:8 109
1:9a 68
1:9–11 .... 22, 27, 124,
              126, 128, 137
1:9b–11 68
1:11 .... 113, 116
1:12 .... 27, 61
1:12–26 .... 22, 27, 39
1:18 62
1:19 .... 61, 139
1:21 118
1:27 39
1:27–30 .... 22, 118
1:27–2:4 39
1:27–2:18 36
1:30 118
2:5 40
2:6–7 39
2:6–8 .... 40, 128, 140,
                     153

2:6–11 ... 36, 38, 40, 139,
        140, 160, 161, 163
2:8 39
2:9–11 .... 39, 40, 141
2:11 .... 125n29
2:12–18 40
2:14 .... 109, 137
2:14–15 138
2:15 138
2:16 .... 125n30
2:19–30 40
2:29a 109
3:17 116
3:19 .... 125n29
3:20 139
3:21 .... 125n29
4:19 .... 125n29
4:20 .... 125n29

Colossians

1:9 .... 62, 64
1:9–12 150
1:11 137
1:15–20 .... 139, 141
1:27 137

1 Thessalonians

1:5 137

1 Timothy

3:16 139
4:11–13 133
4:16 133

2 Timothy

2:15 133

3:14–15 136
3:15 153
3:16–17 .... 9, 134, 158
4:2 134

Hebrews

1:1–4 139
2:11 137
5:7 122
5:11 25
5:11–14 25
6:1 25
6:12 25

1 Peter

4:9 137
5:11 137

2 Peter

1:16 .... 4n5
1:20–21 .... 4n5
3:18 .... 137, 154

1 John

1:6 .... 158n5

Jude

7 122
25 137

Revelation

1:1 117
3:14–22 .... 6n6
3:15–16 .... 6n6
7:4–8 143
7:9–17 143
21:10–27 141

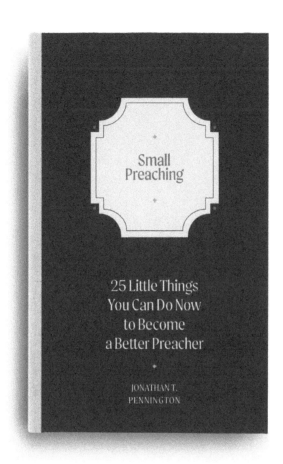

Small
Preaching

25 Little Things
You Can Do Now
to Become
a Better Preacher

JONATHAN T.
PENNINGTON

ALSO AVAILABLE
FROM LEXHAM PRESS

*Small Preaching: 25 Little Things You Can Do
Now to Become a Better Preacher*

———

Visit lexhampress.com to learn more